AFRICAN HISTORY IN THE MAKING

"In the early years after the war the idea began to grow in many minds that educational affairs and policy in Africa needed to be carefully reviewed and in many respects, thought out afresh," writes the Chairman in his Preface to an exhaustive Report of the Cambridge Conference on African Education.

This Conference, held in 1952, was attended not only by representatives of the Colonial Office and the United Kingdom, but also by selected territorial teams representing the colonial territories. And because these territorial teams formed an almost complete cross-section of the educational world of British Africa, and because those present at the Conference—unofficial as well as official members, teachers and administrators, Africans and Europeans, men and women, Christians and Muslims—stated and exchanged their views freely, the findings of the Conference are of extraordinary interest and significance.

In order to place the findings of the Cambridge Conference within easy reach of the non-specialist reader, the Report is here presented in a lively and eminently readable form. "To Canon McLeod Campbell, indeed, the Conference is more than an episode in educational history," writes the Master of Balliol in his Foreword. "It belongs to the history at least of British Africa, and it raises problems of still wider significance, for everyone involved in African affairs must recognize the full implications of the title he has chosen." Facts about the contemporary situation are set against a vivid background picture of the existing physical, cultural and political conditions; the difficulties which confront the present-day educationist in his effort to maintain due regard for tradition, a just appraisement of priorities and a balanced judgment of educational values are imaginatively dealt with.

Two Supplements extend and confirm the author's survey with brief and graphic outlines of past and present educational developments.

AFRICAN HISTORY IN THE MAKING

By

J. McLEOD CAMPBELL, D.D.

Master of Charterhouse, Chaplain to the Queen.
Formerly Principal of Trinity College, Kandy

With a Foreword by The Master of Balliol

LONDON
EDINBURGH HOUSE PRESS
2, EATON GATE, S.W.1

First Published 1956

PRINTED IN GREAT BRITAIN BY
BILLING AND SONS LTD.
GUILDFORD AND LONDON

Contents

v

Foreword

By the Master of Balliol
Chairman of the Advisory Committee on
Colonial Colleges of Arts, Science and Technology

IT is a privilege to be allowed to draw attention to the service which Canon McLeod Campbell has performed in writing this little book. His survey of the proceedings of the 1952 Conference at Cambridge on African education will, I hope, place before a wider public than could have been reached by the original Report the issues discussed in a gathering which, on a theme of outstanding importance, spoke with very special authority; for in its range of membership, and the wealth of responsible experience on which it drew, this Conference formed the most powerful body ever to review the problems of education in British Africa. It had the advantage of being able to direct its debates towards the findings of two admirable reports—the Binns Report on East and Central Africa, and the Jeffery Report on West Africa. Its procedure enabled it to carry out a methodical enquiry into all the main points which these Reports disclosed. Canon McLeod Campbell's book, however, presents much more than a summary of these Reports and discussions; it is a conspectus of the proceedings as a whole, in their relation to the whole of British Africa. The result, as it appears to me, is a work of independent value, an assessment as well as a record of an occasion which may well prove historic in African educational history.

To Canon McLeod Campbell, indeed, the Conference is more than an episode in educational history. It belongs to the history at least of British Africa, and it raises problems of still wider significance, for everyone involved in African affairs must recognize the full implications of the title he has chosen. Educa-

vii

tion is in fact becoming a central theme in the unfolding processes of modern African history; perhaps, indeed, *the* central theme, as it comes to be the chief task and instrument of African government. It is recognized to be the means without which the poverty of Africa cannot be relieved, its resources developed, the health of its people protected, their standard of living raised; without which social transformation will be for the worse and not the better, the political advancement impossible or illusory.

These are heavy tasks. It sometimes seems as though too much were being expected from education in Africa, or anyhow too many things in too short a time. Canon McLeod Campbell's Survey is a corrective to the unrealistic optimism which has prevailed in some quarters during the post-war years. For those who know the facts best optimism, however surely grounded, must be tempered by a cautious appraisal of difficulties; those of language, culture and creed; those of choosing the right methods and providing the right means of instruction; of recruiting and training teachers; of distributing effort between the various forms of education so as to apply limited resources to attainable and worthwhile objects. And yet caution cannot be the main maxim. For while there is much to be done, and much of it the hard way, there is little enough time to do it in. Africa is on the march.

In face of these difficulties, there is one unfailing encouragement. In Africa, unlike certain other regions of the tropical world, no challenge to Western education so far arises from any rival system, ancient or contemporary. The West is still given an open door and a welcome for the best it has to offer. Canon McLeod Campbell's book will help towards the wisest and best use of this opportunity.

D. LINDSAY KEIR.

Preface

THE Queen's visit to Nigeria has put West Africa on the popular map; the voices of African school children welcoming Her Majesty have echoed through every cinema in the British Commonwealth.

A recent Royal Commission has put East Africa on the map. Its Report is a state-paper of historical significance. It proclaims better and more widespread education as "a necessary element, and indeed a prerequisite of a higher standard of living." The Commission endorses at many points the report of the Binns Committee which provided basic material for the Cambridge Conference.

In his *New Hope in Africa* (Longmans, 7s. 6d.), Dr. J. H. Oldham has put Capricorn Africa on the map—Africa within the Tropic of Capricorn, championing the new approach to its problems of the Capricorn Africa Society. This Society which derives its origin from within Africa, and draws its membership from all races, believes that a far richer and greater thing can be achieved by the active co-operation of all the different races than by any more partial approach. It puts its faith in the new outlook of a body of people "who are beginning to think in terms of the total facts and the total good, and are doing their major thinking about public affairs together with members of other races." The Cambridge Conference may be said to have applied this principle and proved its validity in the realm of education.

What that experience was it is the purpose of these pages to register, and rescue from oblivion.

One question was excluded from its terms of reference, What of the higher reaches of African education? A second will suggest itself to the reader, What practical results follow from such a Conference? On both I am able in two Supplements to quote

ix

the evidence of experts. In the first Mr. W. E. F. Ward of the Colonial Office surveys the development of African education over 50 years, ranging from lowly beginnings to University and Higher Technical heights. In the second Mr. J. W. A. Thorburn, who has lately retired from the Nigeria Service, gives his impressions of the advance in Western Nigeria in which he himself played an active part. This account may be taken as very broadly typical of developments in certain other parts of West Africa, notably the Gold Coast and Eastern Nigeria.

To my thanks to these contributors I must add an expression of gratitude for the honour which the Head of my own College has done me in writing a Foreword.

J. McL. C.

Chapter One

THE VERDICT OF POSTERITY

AFRICA will loom large in the perspective of posterity. So much at least it is safe to predict. Self-styled realists may regard the survival of posterity 500 years hence as problematical, but assuming their existence it is to be expected that the historians of the 25th century surveying the 20th century will focus attention on Africa as the high-light of that epoch.

That will be the obvious emphasis for historians bred in the universities of Africa, whose overriding interest will be the emergence of their own continent on a world stage, and the development of its culture. But what of the world historians of A.D. 2500? If such there be they will be the product of a new world order transcending the bounds of this or that country or continent. They will think in terms of a world civilisation presenting infinite diversities corresponding to the various strains in its heredity, but none the less a whole. They will be able to write of it as a whole as British and American historians today can write of their highly composite countries as wholes.

These historians of the future are to be envied, but their lot is not altogether enviable. Their range will be embarrassingly extended. Their material will be overwhelming in bulk compared with that of a 20th-century historian writing of the 15th century. It will not only consist of documentary evidence, but will include visual and aural aids enabling them to scan the features and catch the accents of the principal actors. We may be certain that their perspective will be different from ours. Our "Middle Ages" will not be "Middle" for them, nor our "Modern History" modern.

They are not likely to deny to the 20th century that revolutionary character claimed with pride or self-pity by those who belong to it, but it may be that many of its happenings in Europe, Asia or America will look to them as hang-over from the 19th century and its predecessors, the harvest of seed sown long before.

It is in the emergence of Africa that they will find the distinctive and most significant achievement of the 1900's. An American professor may have been anticipating their view when he said, "The ultimate pivotal stability of the free world lies in Africa." Not that they are likely to isolate African from world history : to understand it they must understand its world context; in the region of events the bearing of world wars, economic developments, scientific discoveries; in the region of ideas the influence of currents of thought, dominant conceptions of nationality and race and religion.

The views of these hypothetical historians will be related to their knowledge of the intervening centuries. The volume of the future which is closed to us will lie open before them. It is in the light of that future that they will judge the 20th century. Posterity is not the final tribunal before whom we shall stand, nor the most merciful, but it is profitable to anticipate its enquiries. They will ask of the 20th century as we ask of the 15th or 18th, what awareness was there of impending change or approaching crisis? Jefferson in the Paris of the 1770's wrote home that he was confining his attention to rural problems, as America would never be anything but an agricultural country. Were there corresponding blind spots in the 20th century's vision of Africa? Was contemporary Africa or contemporary Europe or America taking account of what was coming to birth? Or having come to birth was already growing up? Were they recognizing the potentialities of that Continent? Looking back on 500 years of African history, the story of growing pains, perhaps of adolescent wild-oats, of set-backs and checks, culminating (as we take leave to expect and assume) in an ultimate and glorious maturity, was anything being done, they will ask, at all commensurate with the issues hanging in the balance? What of education? Was there an African appetite for education? Was Africa producing enlightened teachers all up the scale from kindergarten to university? What kind of colleges and schools were in existence? Were there educational authorities concerned with such provision? Were the governments alive to their responsibilities? What obstacles impeded educational progress? Apathy? Inexperience? Expense? Dissensions between and within religious communities? Inadaptability to African needs? Rigid adherence to European models and precedents? Racial and political animosities?

These are questions that posterity is fully entitled to ask. There is no lack of contemporary literature, blue-books, biographies, reports and reviews in which 25th-century historians may find reflected the aspirations, achievements, failures and blunders of 20th-century Africans and Europeans in the sphere of African education. One such contribution to their researches, which it is the purpose of this booklet to spot-light, may serve as a convenient summary of the conditions which confronted educational authorities and enthusiasts in the Africa of 1952.

This is the report of a Conference held in the University of Cambridge in the autumn of 1952, and published under the title "*African Education:* a study of educational policy and practice in British Tropical Africa." Even those who like the writer derive their educational experience from outside Africa will find the story of this Conference arresting. It was notable for two distinctive characteristics, its composition and the thoroughness of its preparatory work.

Taking the second point first, it will be found that the record of what was done at Cambridge is preceded by the reports dealing with East-Central and West Africa respectively on which all discussions were focussed. The Conference was indeed, as its chairman put it, "the culminating event in a long process." There had been general agreement "that educational affairs and policy in Africa needed to be carefully reviewed, and in many respects thought out afresh." The Royal Commission method had been discarded as too formal and impersonal: a more intimate approach was favoured. Two small parties of experienced educational men and women were sent, four to West Africa, three to East Africa, financed by the Nuffield Foundation, sponsored by the Colonial Office, to discuss their educational problems alongside those most intimately concerned, African and

European, official and unofficial, teachers and parents. They were called "Study Groups," and the name connoted something different from courts of enquiry, or inspectors' visitations. Their reports skim the cream of all these friendly conversations, "and supplied the framework round which everything that took place at Cambridge shaped itself." One of them concludes, "Our hopes spring not only from a sense of duty but from the respect and affection for the people of all races whom we found working in the territories we visited." Such was the spirit and the approach of both Study Groups.

The Conference was no less notable for its composition. There were representatives of the Colonial Office (in mufti, for they talked off the record), and of British universities, but the great majority of members were specially selected representatives of fourteen territories. "They came in territorial teams, and formed an almost complete cross-section of the educational world of British Africa." There were officials and non-officials, African and European, men and women, Christian and Muslim, Roman Catholics and non-Roman Catholics, under the chairmanship of the Vice-Chancellor of Bristol University, Sir Philip Morris. "Our chief purpose," he writes, "has obviously been in the field of human relations. Education however efficiently organized, however well administered, and however thorough the methods of instruction, fails of its whole genius and purpose unless it is based upon the relations between individuals, between individuals and groups, and between groups and larger collections of men and women which we call nations, countries and societies. . . . It is the current of human feeling which is the real measure of anything of permanent educational effect. . . . In sessions and outside old friendships were renewed and new ones made. No one who attended the Conference could have left it without a deep impression of a community of purpose. . . . The fact that this extremely various group could not only meet for a common purpose, but also live together in close community for a fortnight, and find itself at once sorry to disperse and delighted to go home and get on with the job is proof that some measure of success was achieved." It was one of the few visitors from outside. Professor Bigelow of Columbia University, who testified to the friendliness of the Cambridge atmosphere and the impression which "the human warmth that has marked our relation with one another" had made upon him.

"If anyone is tempted to say that there is nothing novel, nothing new about education or education in Africa in this report, let him think again" said the chairman in his epilogue. "The assembly in one room of so many and various representatives of so many territories, all of whom brought contributions to a common pool from the considerable resources of educational experience in British Africa, was as new as it was inspiring."

The very fact of such a Conference so composed and preceded by such intensive study, and carried through so harmoniously is the short answer to posterity's main question. It may therefore be thought that at this point "posterity" might be allowed to drop out and the practical problems of the present to come to the fore in their own right. But there may be advantages in retaining "posterity" as a point of reference. First it will be a guide to our selection from a vast mass of material. If we concentrate on what we think will interest posterity the chances are that we shall hit on points that will satisfy the curiosity that we ourselves as intelligent observers are feeling, or ought to be feeling, about what is happening in the educational world of Africa, while others which are the concern of the expert but too technical for the observer will slip into the background.

Secondly a distant point of reference may be useful in lifting delicate and disputable issues out of a polemical atmosphere. It will at any rate be a safer point of reference than the next election, for the introduction of democratic institutions has in some countries embroiled education in arguments that are not primarily educational.

Thirdly, anticipation of the 25th century's cold and ruthless assessment of what the 20th century did or failed to do may jolt us out of complacency, providing a true perspective and correcting errors of proportion, of opportunism, of insular or territorial parochialism.

Chapter Two

AFRICAN APPETITE FOR EDUCATION

POSTERITY'S first question is addressed to the African of the 20th century. Had you as a people any appetite for education? Was there any pressure for education coming from your leaders of public opinion, your parents, your children and youth?

1. The Pressure of Public Opinion

The answer of the children is not in doubt. Jacques's picture in *"As you like it"* of "the whining schoolboy, with his satchel and shining morning face, creeping like snail unwilling to school" does not apply in Africa. "The pupils are eager to learn and apply themselves to their labours with admirable persistence. The problem of class discipline simply does not arise. The dullest lesson, which would produce riot and commotion if inflicted on a class of English children, is received with profound attention." Yet we are told, "Many children have considerable difficulty in getting to school and many quite young children have to travel distances each morning and evening up to ten miles through country where communications are bad and almost impossible at certain seasons. In some areas wild animals are by no means a negligible factor and we heard (in East Africa) of little stragglers from the main body of children who have been picked off by lions or leopards on their way home from school."

In this chapter as in others we confront the dangers of generalisation. There are a thousand Africas. The traditions of countless tribes provide a kaleidoscopic background. The outer world has broken in upon African peoples by differing stages and with varying intensity. Progress towards self-government, central and local, is far from uniform. Between East and West

Africa there are contrasts in the phase of development attained, and within that broad division there are innumerable sub-divisions and cross-divisions, between rural and urban, industrialized and agricultural, between cultures Christian, Muslim and Animist. Nigeria with its 30 millions differs from Gambia, Kenya and Zanzibar or Uganda neighbours. Nevertheless it would not always be possible to tell whether a quotation came from the Eastern or Western Report, whether a contribution to the Cambridge discussions emanated from Nigeria or Uganda. There are resemblances in the two Reports which cannot be put down to coincidence. They reflect factors which affect Africa as a whole and have a close relevance to the question of Africa's appetite for education.

i

Africa in the first place is depicted as Africa-conscious to a degree surpassing even the Asia-consciousness of contemporary Asia, and certainly to a degree unrealisable in earlier centuries, even in earlier decades. External events have had their share in stirring this new sense of "Africa". African troops' participation in distant campaigns has enlarged the horizon. Upheavals resulting from the re-distribution of power in the world and the attainment of independent status for Asian countries have been registered on African seismographs and encourage the expectation of comparable eruptions, of which preliminary tremors have already been felt. But internal events have also awakened a new capacity for seeing the African woods as well as the trees. Africa is no longer dependent on grape-vine telegraphy: wireless and press, railways and lorries and planes make every corner of Africa aware of what is happening in every other corner. What redounds to Africa's glory excites instantaneous jubilation; what is derogatory to Africa's honour sends an instantaneous quiver of indignation throughout the continent. Such new-found awareness of Africa's place in the world-that-is-to-be is one stimulus to educational enthusiasm.

ii

The breathless rapidity of change is another. Education is swept along in its train; developments equally rapid are impatiently demanded. "Economically and socially everything is changing with almost frightening rapidity" reports the Western Study Group; "Even the community life of the rural areas, which often retains an atmosphere of almost Biblical simplicity, is being made aware of the spirit of change by the advent of motor transport and the bicycle and the widespread change to a cash economy. The less isolated areas are being plunged almost at one stride from an agrarian society into the middle of an industrial revolution, while all along the coastal belt problems of evil and suffering, painfully reminiscent of the Industrial Revolution in England, are already engaging the troubled minds of all thinking men and women."

The Eastern Group comments as emphatically on the "speed and intensity of the impact of modern civilization. Civilization is not leaving the African in his ignorance. Africa is on the march. New influences of all kinds are crowding in. If education does not bring the right formative influences to bear, then the wrong ones will have the field all to themselves, and disaster is certain. . . . Whether we like it or not, trade and commerce, the wireless and the cinema and the growth of communications are rapidly altering the whole way of life for Africans."

iii

The reference to the danger of disaster points to a third educational incentive. What is to happen if character cannot keep pace with material opportunity? The onrush of civilization's flood sweeps away many familiar landmarks, social and moral, and society has to reconstruct itself on new foundations. Here again our Western and Eastern authorities are on common ground. In the West "the extended family system has been thrown out of gear, with its delicate balance of rights and obligations, its wide network of relationships and activities which embraced the total life of the community—political, religious, economic and social—and which provided security and legal and moral sanctions of both public and private conduct. Its collapse and inadequacy for the new situation has meant the weakening, and in some cases the breakdown of the moral and legal sanctions of the community."

In East and Central Africa "After at the most eighty years Africans are being expected to move from their social and cultural patterns of living into a version of them that accepts, absorbs, and modifies the influences of Western civilization . . . into a world of thought that covers the Christian way of life, communism, internationalism, and democratic institutions. . . . Here were closely knit, highly organized societies, where the individual subordinated himself in most cases to the group —his family his clan or his age-group. Codes of conduct bound men from the cradle to the grave. . . . Inevitably the coming of a more advanced civilization upsets this pattern and the removal of one set of sanctions is not met with the offer and acceptance of another as detailed and all-embracing in its scope. The tribal moral code had very often a high community value, but civilization with its encouragement to movement of peoples, fresh associations, and new ideas, is rapidly breaking up the tribal structure of the African, and where the collapse of that structure is unaccompanied by education, Africans are in danger of becoming an amoral people." (Amoral is defined in the O.E.D., in contradistinction from immoral, as "not to be characterized as either good or bad : not within the sphere of moral sense.")

iv

The appetite for education grows by what it feeds on. It may be an acquired taste but it is a taste that has been acquired. "Recent times have seen a rapid extension of the educated classes in West Africa. Centering around the older school foundations, there have for a long time been a number of African families educated in successive generations, and their members have provided a small but very influential group in African society." "The achievements of the past show how great are the spiritual resources which can be mobilized for educational effort on the West Coast. . . . Individual Africans have achieved distinction as judges, surgeons, business men, nurses, in the creative arts, and in other walks of life. What is more they have achieved the culture that is the mark of a truly educated person. . . . To all this may be added the achievement of Africans in the skilled trades whenever sound instruction has been provided. The potentialities of the West African have been demonstrated by actual achievement."

V

Appetite is further whetted by the need, if Africa is to realize its destiny, to train African leaders in all walks of life. "By 1952 education was in a condition of headlong change and development. Some 2,750 African students (many of them on scholarships provided from public funds) were studying in the universities and other higher training establishments in the United Kingdom, and some hundreds more in the United States and Canada."* "The problem of African society as of all other societies is rooted in the need for leadership, and training in that social responsibility without which the expenditure of large sums on development of all kinds will not produce a workable constitution or a better society."

2. Parental Opinion

So far we have only dealt with posterity's question as it affects those who have themselves been educated and are trained to think in terms of the community. Is the appetite for education confined to the politically conscious? What of the rank and file? The parents of Africa? Do they share this appetite for education, and what whets it?

It will be in keeping with the Conference's obvious desire to be realistic and scrupulous avoidance of exaggeration if we marshall such facts or symptoms that might seem to dictate a negative answer.

It is not for example claimed that the appetite for education is universal. There are areas in which a few schools suffice to meet the demand, where it is still difficult to persuade people to send their children to school. This is enough of a problem for the Conference to discuss what to do when one area is clamouring for more schools than can be given it while another is apathetic. "The tendency has been to try and force schools on the backward area and to tell the progressive area that it must wait until the others have had their fair share."

A second misgiving arises from the "wastage", which

* By 1956 this number had increased to 5,390.

shocked and haunted the Eastern Study Group. Parents are suspected of condoning truancy, and their appetite for education is
too easily assuaged by incomplete courses that "are a complete
waste of the child's time and their money."

It is in the sphere of girls' education that parental appetite is
thought to require some stimulating. "The education of women
lags seriously behind that of men." The Conference discussed
"the initial problem of persuading public opinion in Africa that
girls of school age should be released from the heavy burden of
domestic drudgery and allowed to enter the schools. We must
face the fact that until this drudgery is diminished by labour-
saving devices such as power-driven mills or pipe-borne water,
parents will have to make real sacrifices both in money and in
labour, in dispensing with a daughter's services."

Resistance may go deeper than that. "Women themselves
are sometimes the strongest opponents of change. They fear the
effect of contact with Europeans for their daughters and the
result of education upon them. . . . Education comes as a dis-
ruptive force. It excludes groups of girls from the community,
and thus saps the power of the older women, and this isolation
tends to make them outcasts who suffer loneliness until a sufficient number can make a society of their own. African women,
who cannot rest from the daily round of labour on which the
life of the community depends, develop a sense of duty and of
responsibility to a greater degree than most men. They
genuinely believe that if they were relieved of their burdens
they would be betraying their trust as wives and mothers as
they see it, and this explains again their dislike and distrust of
the effects of education. It must be recognized that the modern-
ization of women's life may lead to a temporary set-back both in
their status and their influence in society. The removal of the
old externally imposed discipline may result in moral decline
unless self-restraint takes its place based upon a positive code
of behaviour rooted in spiritual belief."

The prospect of a yawning gulf between illiterate parents and
sophisticated children may cause legitimate apprehension. As
Lord Hailey wrote in his *African Survey* : "Education in Africa
is an instrument of change and not as in more static communities an instrument for maintaining the continuity of culture;

when the African child is perforce introduced to a world of thought, achievement and of conduct outside the experience of his parents, this access to new ideas is bound to make a break in his life, however much the educationist may wish to respect native tradition." Wherever children are being introduced to ways of looking at life at variance with the outlook that has been hallowed by centuries of tradition a gulf opens which, if not bridged by understanding teachers, threatens the cohesion of family and tribe.

There comes a point too when the number of the schooled multiplies and the young turn away from the land to an extent that seems to threaten the very existence of the community. "As one enlightened chief put it, 'If universal primary education were introduced at once, Sierra Leone would be dead in a year, we would starve.' A rapid increase in numbers would and does threaten the stability of the community by withdrawing essential labour from the land and by turning out from the schools more boys expecting outside employment than there is employment for."

It is against this background of understandable anxieties, aggravated sometimes by bad teachers or the perils of the road to and from school, that the avidity for education stands out in such astonishing intensity. East and West corroborate one another's testimony on this point. "The interest in education is very widespread and by no means confined to the teaching profession and the educational service. Educational questions are discussed everywhere and indeed in some parts education takes the foremost place in political policy and propaganda." Such political pressure may be a menace exposing education to its detriment to the influence of non-educational factors, but its existence is one answer to the question whether there is an appetite for education. It is strong enough to exert constant pressure on the educational authorities to go faster than they think is wise and to sacrifice quality to quantity—to open more schools than they can staff. "Over the greater part of these territories," to quote the Eastern report, "there is a sincere and earnest demand for the benefits of education. Sometimes this demand is almost passionate in its nature and there is intense grief and disappointment when a child fails to gain admission to a school. Often parents make great sacrifices to send their children to school, and often communities spontaneously offer to tax themselves to pay for the education of their people, and voluntarily give money or labour to put up classrooms. Some local authorities have become almost bankrupt owing to the extent to which they have drawn on their resources to pay for local schools." "Though emancipated women are often resented, there is a growing conviction among responsible Africans that the future of their peoples depends upon the existence of a sound proportion of educated women." The conclusion is that "the time has gone by when missions and administrators offered education to an indifferent people. Now parents demand far more schools than the Government can supply."

The fact is that the distinction drawn between the politically conscious and the rank and file of the people can be overdrawn. By and large all Africans are politically conscious, and would give very much the same answer to the question, What whets the appetite for education? "There is everywhere and among all sections of the population a desire to see a rapid expansion of the educational system: Africans are often ready to go without material advantages if their children can be educated; those concerned with economic development in every department want a rapidly increasing number of educated men and women for their work so that standards of living may be raised, and all those engaged in social and welfare services need many recruits to advance their work."

If the African parent were asked to analyse his or her motives, the answer might excusably take the form of a "tu quoque." What are your motives as a British parent for straining every nerve to secure the best education you can for your children? Comparative analysis would probably bring to light a not dissimilar mixum-gatherum of motives, some more healthy than others which carry some taint of snob and social climber, but the healthier predominating, and inspiring genuine sacrifice and disinterested ambition.

Chapter Three

THE TEACHING PROFESSION IN AFRICA

POSTERITY'S second question like the first is addressed to Africans. We want to know, they say, whether your Africa of 500 years ago was breeding teachers of quality in sufficient numbers to lay the foundations on which later centuries could build? What was the status of the teaching profession in your days? What were you doing to ensure that your teachers were so well trained that at every level from kindergarten to university enlightened men and women were in action? A story has come down to us of the Scottish head of a training establishment who was making a round of his old students accompanied by an African colleague. He found one who was showing remarkable initiative in a not altogether conventional way, and he turned to his colleague to ask his opinion as to the soundness of the new methods. The reply was "I can't remember." Not having his notes with him he could not turn up the answer. Is that at all characteristic of the men you were training? Were they all rule-of-thumb teachers, applying in practice what they had learnt by rote? We would like reassurance too on the other two counts. We have a tradition that in your day the best men and women were being diverted from the vocation of teaching to other alluring and more lucrative callings, and that the prestige of the teaching profession stood a long way below par.

If the enquirers of A.D. 2452 refer to *African Education* issued in A.D. 1952, they will find that its contributors recognized the primacy of their three questions, and were not altogether happy about any of them. A large share of the reports and discussions is devoted to them. They were brutally frank in exposing weaknesses when they found them and ruthless in prescribing remedies.

24

These three questions of the supply, the status, and the training of teachers overlap, being closely inter-related, but they can most conveniently be treated separately.

1. *Supply*

If Africa cannot produce her own teachers no question arises; the whole educational edifice must crumble for nobody can do it for her. However much men and women from outside Africa may be welcomed under the polite soubriquet of "expatriates", they can never be numerous enough to sustain so immense an enterprise.

There is no lack of appreciation of what African teachers of all ranks have achieved, often in the face of heavy odds—inadequate buildings and equipment, premature withdrawal of pupils, and their own premature transfers, exacting double sessions, discouragement of initiative, cramping rigidity of method, and curricula irrelevant to life. Children through no fault of their own are not always in teachable condition, and there are many interruptions. "Where an older child leaves school younger brothers or sisters cannot come unescorted, and so the education of the older ceases or is broken until the younger are old enough to come alone. Then there are the seasonal demands of planting and harvesting, of herding cattle, or of animal and bird scaring which break up regular attendance. In many areas there are hunger months when children cannot come to school because they are too weak, or are hunting for food, or come too debilitated to learn. Then there are the home duties night and morning which tire the children. Girls suffer particularly in the share they take from early childhood in household responsibilities." All this aggravates the difficulties of class-teaching and the teacher's lot if not an unhappy one is handicapped. African teachers and headmasters have not been daunted.

"There are schools which are right ahead of current practice in their own area which serve at once as a model and an inspiration. Sometimes such an outstanding school will develop from the vision and drive and determination of a headmaster without any outside encouragement or specially favoured treatment. Anyone who visits schools must have come across that amazing power which can inspire a collection of mediocre individuals and weld them into an outstanding staff producing as a team results which seem far beyond the reach of any of its individual members."

It is the supply of such teachers which is causing anxiety. "In most parts of the West Coast educational expansion is being slowed down by lack of teachers, while in all parts the education being provided is far less effective than it should be because the majority of teachers have not the training and qualifications necessary for a full appreciation of their responsibilities."

"In the early stages of a rapidly developing educational system there is a period of very real conflict. To set a standard of education and training for teachers high enough to avoid the likelihood of the blind being led by the partially sighted would so restrict the opening of new schools as to produce acute political pressure. To allow the unrestricted opening of schools may well involve such a dilution of the profession with the semi-educated and untrained that all real educational values are forgotten in a headlong pursuit of literacy. The Accelerated Development Plan for Education in the Gold Coast faces the dilemma in an acute form. It promises primary school education to all children of the appropriate age in Ashanti and the Colony, whose parents desire it for them. This is a decision of the people properly taken through their constitutional and democratic forms of government." The problem of recruiting teachers assumes embarrassing proportions. "The question is no longer whether it is possible to find the required number with qualifications up to an approved standard, but what kind of teachers will be forthcoming in the required number, and what kind of training can be given to them in the time available. For many years the standards of the profession must fall short of what by any criterion could be regarded as adequate . . . but if the means proposed in the Plan are energetically pursued and if nothing is allowed to diminish or postpone the plans for training in the future, there is no reason why there should not be steady and progressive upgrading of the teaching profession from within."

"Since teachers are the product of schools you cannot have teachers until you have schools or schools until you have teachers. You cannot have good schools until you have good teachers or good teachers until you have good schools . . ." "But a vicious circle may sometimes be converted into a spiral. Anything that can be done to get more good teachers into West African schools will pay immediate dividends in the improvement of the schools and deferred dividends in the improvement of the teachers of the next generation."

Teachers cannot be blamed if they do not rise above the level of their source. "At present recruitment is almost always from the senior primary or middle school, and this is probably inevitable for some time to come, but the aim should certainly be recruitment from the secondary school." Happily "the standard from which teachers are being trained is steadily rising throughout East and Central Africa: the lower standards which had been thought sufficient for women teachers are disappearing thanks to the immense improvement in the general education of girls."

It cannot be denied that there are at present shortages of teachers in most territories, "but these shortages would almost certainly be overcome if the conditions of service offered to teachers were sound. . . . It has been the very strong impression formed from many meetings with teachers and school-children who intend to take up teaching that, in fact, there is at present a great desire on the part of many Africans to play a part in the educational progress of their own people. Their motives may be mixed, but there is a generous measure of sincere altruism and religious belief; they realize that education means material and spiritual enlightenment for their compatriots. Among some people this zeal for education with consequent ambition to enter the teaching profession is enormously strong. This makes it all the more necessary that unsatisfactory conditions of service should not deter individuals or frustrate genuine conviction among groups of Africans." This quotation provides a bridge to our next division of the subject.

2. *Status*

We may take a text here from the West African report. "The problem of African education can only be solved if the status and standing of the teaching profession is unquestioned and if teachers become jealous of their high professional integrity."

The point is developed later in the same report. "The immediate problem is to secure for teaching a due proportion of the best material in the primary schools. Unfortunately this aim is far from realization. Evidence that teaching is at present fairly low on the list of desirable occupations is too widespread to be ignored. The remuneration and conditions of service must be made more attractive than they are at present. It is rare for a candidate to seek admission to a Training College until he has tried and failed to gain admission to a secondary school. . . . The tendency on every count is for the teaching profession and even for that part of it which is trained, to be recruited from the less able and less devoted young Africans."

Africa is not the only country where the list of "desirable occupations" lengthens to the detriment of the teaching profession—occupations attractive and satisfying as combining usefulness to the community with dignity of status, and prospects sometimes dazzlingly lucrative. Many such occupations can put in a weighty claim for the best recruits, for men who can be counted on to put community before career and scorn to feather their own nests. Yet a country incurs reproach if it is so short-sighted as to load the dice against its teaching profession by offering deterrent terms of service. A man cannot be condemned as mercenary if a legitimate sense of injustice casts a blight on his service. It may be a disparity between the rewards accorded to the teaching as compared with other professions. It may be disparity within the profession itself. Both these are admitted by the Cambridge Conference to be genuine grievances.

"We are satisfied that in some territories teachers are materially worse off during their training than recruits for other government departments, which must prove disastrous in the long run, for it will result in the second-best becoming teachers, who are likely to be much more expensive in the long run than the first-rate. Teachers' salaries should be on a par in all respects with the salaries paid to officers of other government departments of the same training and qualifications."

These sentiments will be applauded by Teachers' Associations in many other parts of the world, however novel it may be to them to hear teachers alluded to as civil servants—a status they may have been accustomed to repudiate as derogatory to the profession's integrity.

"The discrepancy between salary scales for teachers and those which apply to 'other civil servants' of similar qualifications and length of training cause a lower grade of candidate to enter the profession. In five territories of East and Central Africa teachers' salaries are equated as nearly as possible with the corresponding posts in the civil service. In the two where they are not there is the greatest evidence of discontent among the teachers. Where special cost-of-living allowances should be made to civil servants corresponding allowances should be made to teachers, as well as corresponding arrangements for sick-pay."

Disparity within the profession may also breed discontent; there is for example no pension scheme for teachers in some territories, while in others pensions can be earned by teachers in government and local authority schools but not by those in church schools.* There may also be a wounding disparity between African and European salaries, and it is to counteract this that one Study Group thinks it would be "more appropriate if there were a single scale applicable to African and European alike, Europeans receiving an additional expatriate allowance." But there are also "anomalies existing between the salaries and conditions of service found among different types of school." The Conference endorsed the view that these should be removed, and "all qualified teachers whether teaching in government, local government, voluntary agency or other assisted schools should be on the same scale and subject to the same conditions of service in such matters as leave, housing, pensions, and dismissal." It strongly approved the prevailing trend towards the establishment of a unified teaching service, understanding by this term complete parity of conditions of service financial and otherwise between all teachers of equivalent qualifications.

Teachers' Associations

Prestige however is not something that can be claimed still

* Great efforts are being made in Africa to redress these disparites.

less contended for; it must be earned and conceded spontaneously to merit, to be worth having at all. Self-consciousness about it has ruined many a good teacher and not a few Teachers' Associations. It is to the latter that the Conference looked to enhance most effectively the status of the teaching profession. "The teachers themselves, conscious of their membership of a united and honourable profession, can exert a powerful influence on the development of education. It is most encouraging to find that teachers in West African territories are developing their organisations with all the marks of a good profession —a sense of social purpose, the establishment of high standards of professional conduct, and a regard for the quality and training of those who enter its membership. . . . They are concerned, and rightly, with questions of remuneration and conditions of service, but they are not preoccupied with these to the exclusion of matters touching their professional responsibility. Some of them are already regarded by the authorities and the public as trustworthy organs for the expression of the corporate view of teachers on educational issues. They are a healthy and important element in the educational affairs of West Africa."

The Conference itself shed its benediction on such ventures. It was impressed with the value of a good Teachers' Association in raising the cultural and professional standards of its members. "Aristotle thought that the State is brought into existence to make life possible, but it continues in existence to make life worth living. Similarly the Conference thought that a Teachers' Association is brought into existence to secure better salaries and material conditions for its members; but it continues in existence to help its members to improve their cultural life. A good Association will run libraries, refresher courses and summer schools, will set up professional committees to gather and give expression to its members' opinions on professional matters, and will seek all ways of assisting its members to become better teachers."

The service of such Associations is not the only activity in which teachers are encouraged to engage outside the classroom. "While the teacher's first duty is to his pupils, teachers in Africa form such a large proportion of the small body of educated citizens that their help is needed in public affairs." It is as the teaching fellowship accepts its role in the life of the community that its status in the public regard is assured. (See p. 70.)

3. *Training*

"What were you doing to ensure that your teachers were so well trained that at every level from kindergarten to university enlightened men and women were in action?"

If the proportion of space allotted both by the Study Groups and in the Conference records to Teacher Training Colleges is any indication of the importance attached to them in the Africa of the 1950's, the historian of the future may rest assured that the question he raises did not go unasked or unanswered. He may not be interested in the more technical questions discussed by the experts—problems of size, location, staff, curriculum and the like, but he (and indeed the intelligent observer of to-day) will want to know that the importance of training institutions was appreciated, and that they were being developed in close relation to the growth of the new Africa, and multiplied in proportion to the demands of that growth.

Looking at the present from a distant future our inspector of 500 years hence may not find it easy to make all the allowances for Training College defects and weaknesses that our reporters feel it fair to make. He may not realize the extreme youth of Africa's educational system, and the infancy of its Training College system. *African Education* is merciful in the matter of statistics, but a few figures which it supplies from Nigeria serve to illustrate the rapidity of growth in the 35 years between 1912 and 1947. We have added the corresponding figure for 1951. (See p. 114, Supplement B.)

	1912	*1947*	*1951*
Number of Primary Schools	150	6,094	9,499
Primary School Pupils ...	35,716	538,391	1,002,583
Secondary School Pupils ...	67	9,908 (including 786 girls)	24,225
Teachers-in-Training ...	12	3,786 (including 145 girls)	7,200

It is not surprising that developments so recent and rapid should be reflected in current imperfections in the Training College system. It is not claimed that the human material with whom Training College staffs are entrusted are the best product of the schools: as later study of the educational programme will show there is an awkward gap between school-leaving age and Training College entry age; as the age of entry to schools is lowering an increasing number of pupils will complete their course at 13 or 14, far too young to begin an ordinary training course, nineteen being accepted as the minimum age at which anyone should be allowed to qualify as a teacher. "Some means must be found of filling this gap. Promising material is already being lost because of it." Until such time as a secondary school course is provided for all intending teachers "the Training College must for many students take the place of the secondary school which has been denied to them, striving to fulfil for its students the requirements that those who would be educators must first be educated."

This inevitably overcrowds the curriculum and diverts energy from that strictly vocational training which it is the primary purpose of a Training College to provide. "A College must prepare its students for their future work as teachers by leading them to think about education in an adequate way, by giving them a grounding in the principles on which good teaching is based, by instructing them in the craft of teaching, and showing them in practice what lively and inspired teaching can accomplish. This important part of its work may be approached in different ways according to the capacities of the students. For some it may be approached through philosophical studies of educational principles and psychology, and the analysis of teaching method. For others it is best approached in a simpler and more empirical way. The problems of education are very deep problems, but they are human problems, and can be profitably discussed in simple and non-technical language. Most of the differences between good and bad teaching are fairly obvious to one who has seen good teaching in operation. It is far more important that a man should come to know good teaching by acquaintance than that he should be able to explain what it is in philosophical language."

"Everywhere the old idea of education as a continuous process of imparting information in regular yearly blocks, to be repeated if not absorbed, is giving place to the idea of different types of schools related to the needs of the child and the needs of society. . . . Great advances have been made as a result of researches into child development and methods of learning. . . . These call for the production of a new type of teacher, and this puts the Training Colleges in a key position in relation to development. They should be ahead of general school practice so that it may be regarded as a healthy thing if serving teachers are critical of the new ideas that newly qualified teachers bring with them from their colleges."

All this implies adequate and enlightened tutors and lecturers; the Conference adopted as its definition of adequacy a ratio of staff to students of one to twelve. "We were depressed with the reports we heard of the difficulty of staffing Training Colleges. We were told that they have teachers on their staff who have no vocation for teacher-training; that teacher-training is unpopular; that few of the staff are adequately experienced or qualified for this particular type of work; that governments insist on graduates (whereas half the teachers in British Training Colleges are non-graduates), and often seem content with a graduate without inquiring if he is specially suitable."

This confirms the somewhat gloomy view of the Western Group on the same subject. "The majority of the Training College lecturers are African: there can be no doubt of the importance of their work, and it is vital that this work should attract and retain a fair proportion of the best teachers. Unfortunately it does not at present appear to be doing so. Secondary school work is almost universally preferred, and in many places an able teacher looking for promotion would not think of Training College work until he had given up hope of obtaining a secondary school post or a primary school headship."

Again the youth of the service accounts for haphazard siting of Training Colleges, and great disparities in size. All but ten of the seventy-six Training Colleges included in the Nigerian statistics are under the auspices of "Voluntary Agencies", each church or mission making its independent contribution to the training of teachers as its own circumstances and geography

C

dictate. Hence a somewhat promiscuous dispersal of energy that does not always make for efficiency or economy. Elaborate arguments can be marshalled in favour of large or small colleges respectively. They are fairly presented by the Conference, but whereas the Nigerian average has been shown to be 50 the Conference comes down dogmatically in favour of a minimum 120 and a maximum 200. As to site, the ideal for East-Central Africa is that "a Training College should be so situated that a real love of the countryside can be linked with a proper understanding of the relationship of town and country life."

The Conference was aware that "one of the biggest difficulties facing the Training College is the dead weight of tradition. Head teachers and senior colleagues often fail to understand or sympathise with a young teacher's ideas. Trained teachers often teach by the bad methods they were taught at school, not by the good methods they were taught at college. Even tutors of Training Colleges sometimes dictate notes instead of teaching in ways they would wish their students to imitate. To counteract such blemishes, the Conference advocated better demonstration schools under the control of the College.

"But much more than this will be needed to throw off the dead weight of traditional methods of teaching. . . . It is not enough for a Training College to send its students out into the schools and leave them to their head teachers and inspectors. The College staff must visit the head teachers and invite them to visit the college; the two parties must plan their co-operation. Furthermore just as a model or pilot school would quicken education in each area, concentrating some good trained teachers under an experienced head, so would much benefit be disseminated by Pilot Training Colleges, better equipped and staffed than the average, which could lend specialist staff or equipment to other colleges in turn, and conduct experiments and research."

In spite of realistic judgments it is on the Training Colleges that Conference hopes are fixed for the future of African education, and therefore of Africa. "Here as in so many instances it is in the Teachers' Training Colleges that the ultimate remedy is to be found." "As in most of our recommendations the Teachers' Training Colleges must make a major contribution. . . ." "The Teachers' Training Colleges are in a key position. . . ." Such sentences recur at frequent intervals, testifying to a faith unshaken by disappointments. All were agreed at all costs to "expand and consolidate the provision of those stages of education from which entrants to the Training Colleges are drawn, and that where existing Training College facilities are inadequate the expansion of those facilities should be the next priority. If this involves the necessity of recruiting more expatriate staff until sufficient trained African staff are available, *they should be recruited.*"

Chapter Four

EDUCATIONAL AXIOMS

BEFORE we answer posterity's next question about Africa's educational equipment in 1952 there is a necessary preamble. The fundamental principles must be clarified, and any distinctive ideals or emphases noted. What answer does Africa give to certain test questions which perplex educational planners the world over, and are quite likely to be perplexing them 500 years hence? Such for example are the questions of the diffusion of education, the language of education, the acclimatisation, the spiritual roots of education. Great differences distinguish country from country, century from century, but the experience of one country or century is relevant to that of others, and the assumptions accepted as axiomatic by the educational builders of 20th-century Africa need understanding if the superstructure is to be seen in due perspective.

1. *Diffusion of Education*

It would for example be a serious misunderstanding if it were assumed that African attention was fixed exclusively on the formal education associated with institutions and the classroom, on questions of curricula, time-tables, certificates, examinations, pedagogical gadgets and tricks of the trade. Very early in its survey the Western Group devotes a chapter to what it likes to call "Informal Education". The Eastern Group gives about a tenth of its sections to what it prefers to call "Adult Education". At the Conference itself one of its five subdivisions is wholly concerned with "Education and the Adult". There can be few educational surveys which give the diffusion of education so integral a place in its thinking and policy.

It was indeed from Africa that the original impetus towards "Mass Education" derived. The Colonial Office Report published

under that title in 1944 was related to African experience.
There were two good reasons which account for this emphasis.
Nowhere more than in Africa does the gulf which must always
exist between generations threaten to develop under the erosive
effects of educational flood into an impassable chasm, to the
dividing asunder of homes. "Neglect of this part of the educational programme is both unimaginative and wasteful, since it
has been established that in every society it is impossible to
educate a child far in advance of his parents without creating
serious emotional tensions."

That is the point of view of seniors, self-conscious about their
own illiteracy, but juniors too are deeply affected by the
strength or weakness of available informal education. There
are not enough opportunities of formal education to go round,
and the informal is all too often their only hope of getting any
education at all. Even for the minority who do reach schools,
schooling ends when adolescence has barely begun, and they
too must depend on informal education if their meagre gains
are to be conserved, and their minds are to go on growing.

Many names are used to describe informal education—adult,
mass, welfare education, campaigns for mass literacy, or community development. Unesco calls it "Fundamental". They
cover all forms of educational activity "carried on in any progressive community outside the immediate responsibility of
parents for their children or schools for their pupils; whether
by official or voluntary agency, by individuals or by co-operative
groups. It may be directed towards people of any age and of all
ages, towards people generally or a special class such as parents.
It may have as its object the enrichment of personal life, the
improvement of the methods of performing the daily task, or
the spread of valid ideas of personal probity and social responsibility." "By reason of its informality this kind of education is
flexible and adaptable and has great possibilities in a developing situation such as that in Africa."

Everyone who has been properly educated knows that his
education has only begun when he leaves school or college, and
must be a continuing process all through life. The educated
African will agree that what the Conference stigmatized as "the
ballroom-cum-ping-pong-cum-politics approach" is not satisfy-

ing. If isolated from centres of population where he could continue his self-education by reading and by joining adult societies of various kinds he will look to the Adult Education movement for help in his own self-development. He will also find in it a field of activity in which to express his instincts for community service.

It was indeed its role in community-building that stirred the imagination of the writers of the original Mass Education report: "The stage is set for the conception of a common citizenship which begins to acquire reality and expression. This common citizenship is not to be envisaged as a benevolent conception from above; it is the practical outcome of a common control and common effort." "Means must be found and found quickly whereby the people, *as a community* can understand and appreciate the forces which have changed and are changing their lives so radically. . . . The mass education of the community is a problem of an urgency that is necessitated both by the natural ripening of general problems, and by the forced pace at which those problems social, political and economic are maturing." Acceleration was the keyword; the "community as a whole" the recurring refrain.

That point of view, the community point of view, is shared by the Cambridge Conference. The discussion in Group E on "Education and the Adult" reads as the liveliest of all the discussions; not from its polemical character, for there was no difference of opinion except on a question of administration, namely: Who should be the responsible authority for controlling and stimulating education for literate and illiterate adult? Some voted for the Education Department, some for the Welfare or Community Development Department, some for an inter-departmental authority on which medical, agricultural and other departments would pull their weight. It was the intensity of feeling on the need for adult education that lent colour to the debate.

"It is an urgent matter in my territory because we have so few children at schools and such a dead weight of ignorance to contend with among the adult population." "In my country we have the problem of the great influx of workers into new industries: they cannot be influenced by schools and unless we bring some educational influence to bear on them we risk nothing less than the disintegration of society."

"It will do no good to have the new influence of the schools and the old influence of tradition blindly opposed to one another. Adult Education is the only hope of bringing about a reconciliation."

"The adult literacy campaign brings more children into the schools. Parents who have themselves learnt to read appreciate more the value of schooling for their children."

"The great value of community development is that it gives the African even in the smallest unit of society a chance of organizing himself, and of carrying out his own plans of betterment. Local government comes alive when local government from beneath ties up with local government imposed as at present from a higher level."

The Group made no attempt to write a treatise on a subject covering such a varied field of activity, "that has not yet had time to develop its own orthodoxies," but it carried the whole Conference with it in support of what was acclaimed "the most revolutionary sentence spoken during the conference, and strikingly significant when enunciated by a body of professional educators": revolutionary because in a country so inadequately equipped with conventional educational facilities, it would be understandable if the multiplication of primary and secondary schools was given priority; significant because the members of the Cambridge Conference were professionally concerned with school and college education and yet proclaimed that if necessary the expansion of school and college education must be slowed down to release resources in staff and money for the development of informal education for adults.

"At least for the short term, there should be a quite novel concentration of energy and resources upon the tasks of informal education."

2. *The Language of Education*

The distinctive characteristic of Africa's treatment of so

thorny a subject as the linguistic medium of education is that it was found not to be thorny. The adoption of the English medium does not appear to arouse the emotions stirred by the subject in some parts of the Commonwealth. It is not an issue at elections. The respective shares of the vernacular and English in the student course is treated as a strictly educational problem. There are reasons for this.

No one is more alive than the African to the danger of whatever in his academic studies may estrange Africa's sons and daughters from the realities of African life. He has songs, stories, nursery rhymes, folk tales, proverbs in the vernaculars which must not be allowed to go by the board. There are African arts valued not only by the African but as part of the world's heritage. But Africa is not rich in written records, and few of the vernaculars are widely enough spoken to promise or possess a literature: the position therefore is not analogous to that of Asian cultures.

Africa too stands in need of a lingua franca, for her tongues are legion. No African vernacular would be universally acceptable as having roots in any such ancient cultural and spiritual tradition, as Asian vernaculars have. The language problem thus reduces itself to comparatively simple proportions, dual, not multiple, the exception being Somaliland, where English (without apparently serious detriment to its acquisition) takes third place to Somali and Arabic; and Zanzibar, where Arabic is an additional subject of study. (Arabic is begun as a written language in the second year, but is only used as a spoken language in religious instruction.)

There are variations of policy in different territories on the timing of language study. "On the necessity for the progression from the vernacular at the beginning of the course to English at the end there is little controversy, but over the stages by which this progression should be accomplished there is much argument and great need for experiment and research." In these details we cannot expect the 25th century to be interested, but it will always be interesting to know whether the English language extirpated vernaculars by deliberate and arbitrary policy, or whether its adoption was achieved by common consent.

The answer is that if African vernaculars do not survive into the 25th century it will not be for want of due reverence being paid to them. True there will be casualties. "The new flux and movement of African life is now destroying some vernaculars and blurring others. If the attempt is made to preserve all vernaculars all will be lost. There must be some selection of those in which systematic training is given in a standardized orthography in all schools and colleges. More vernaculars should continue to be studied up to School Certificate standard; and that there may be a sufficient supply of teachers qualified to provide such study there should be a School of African Languages at Makerere. There should be continued study of the vernaculars in which systematic training is given in a standardized ortho-subject called 'African Studies' in which language is linked with music, drama, history and dance."

It may be hoped therefore that there will be no general massacre of languages for the historian of the future to mourn. The explanation will be that Africa in the 20th century recognised that for the building up of her new life she needed both vernacular and English education. "To preserve the vernacular languages of Africa is to preserve the tribes that speak them, and to strengthen the moral sanctions that rest on tribal membership. If a distinctive African contribution is to be made to the world it must be based on the African's love and respect for the mental inheritance of his people, and much of this is enshrined in language. Learning a foreign language in the early stages is necessarily an imitative and memorising process and may encourage an imitative rather than a creative habit of mind. . . . The mother-tongue is the most potent to awaken the dawning imagination; it touches the heart as well as the head. Unless the study of the vernacular is given its right importance another cause will be added to those which tend to uproot the African without giving him a firm footing in a new and stable society."

But Africans want English too. Movements of population enhance the need of a lingua franca. "Africans are avid to secure the technical knowledge and skill which will, they hope, raise them out of poverty and the ever-present fear of drought and famine, and they know that this knowledge in any amount is only available to the man who can read English. Thirdly the knowledge of English introduces the student to the vast store-house of English literature—indeed of world literature, for more foreign books are translated into English than into any other language. Again broadcasting and films can only be fully en-joyed by those who understand English."

It is an interesting claim—and one wonders how it will look 500 years hence!—that "the African needs English today in the same sense and to the same degree as the Renaissance English-man needed Greek or Greek thought in Latin forms. English thought could come to Africa with all the liberating power of Greek thought to Europe." England's experience of 400 years ago when outside influences swept in from abroad not to the submerging but to the revivification of her own traditions of art and literature and its expression in her native idiom may yet be paralleled in Africa.* The Cambridge Conference Group which specialized on this subject records that "a large majority of our Group, including all our African members, feels strongly that the teaching of English should have priority, and that in the long run this will not prove detrimental to the development of vernacular languages large enough to evolve a literature of their own."

3. Education and the Soil of Africa

Is education rooted in the soil of Africa or is it to be classed among exotics that are not likely to acclimatize? They may produce showy blooms and luscious fruit, but they soon grow exhausted by the struggle with adverse influences, and wither. What is the survival value of education?

The question has been treated metaphorically in discussing the future of African languages, but for many including not a few of the Cambridge company it is not a metaphorical ques-tion at all; it must be taken literally and answered in terms of agriculture. Education, it is argued, to fulfil its function and fructify, must be intimately related to the environment in

---

* cf. quotation by A. L. Rouse in his *The Expansion of Elizabethan England:* "Never had Welsh grammar, Welsh prosody, Welsh antiquities received greater attention than during the centuries that witnessed the Anglicising policy of the Act of Union; and that at the hands of the very men who were most receptive of the wider influences of the age." F. Jones, *An Approach to Welsh Genealogy.*

which a person is to spend his life; for the vast majority that environment will be rural; Africa must always depend on agriculture for the livelihood of her people, and for the increased food supply needed by rapidly increasing populations. Unless productivity is increased some of these populations are in danger of famine in the near future, and even now pass annually through "hunger months." The test of a soundly acclimatised education is whether it succeeds in inspiring societies based on sound economy and providing social amenities, and outlets for a wide variety of aptitudes and occupations, in which people can become good citizens and develop their talents.

The prevailing drift to the towns is taken as a symptom of an unacclimatised education, and likely to reproduce many of the evils associated with 19th-century drift to the towns in Great Britain. These evils take on a sinister aspect peculiar to Africa in the eyes of those who believe that "the land and industries based on the land will be the condition of survival as well as the source of wealth of most territories."

There are no doubt other tests of acclimatisation, and the Conference was not unmindful of that "most important minority which will move away from a purely agricultural environment to the growing centres of administration and commerce. It is these who as they come to occupy increasingly important posts in education, the Civil Service and economic development can make the new towns of Africa spearheads in the advance of civilization. The aim of education is to enable every man and woman to lead the most complete life that the environment allows." The acceptance of this principle means that "education in administration and technology must keep pace everywhere with developing opportunities. New minerals and new sources of power will be discovered which will give a great impetus in urban and industrial development, and education must be related to this possibility."

There were those at the Conference who defended the drifter-townward in some circumstances, on the ground that far too many farms are too small to be efficient; if productivity is to be increased there must be large-scale consolidation of small farms into larger. "It would not be enough if the spread of education impelled more educated people to remain on the land to scratch a living out of an uneconomically small plot. We need an agrarian revolution." "Farming must be made more stable and more rewarding through mechanisation possibly on a co-operative basis, with improvement of marketing and distribution.

In the Cambridge discussions the Group hinted at criticism based on misunderstanding, "as if we wanted all pupils to remain on the land." Certainly every possibility is explored to ensure that whatever their future occupation all students in primary, in secondary schools, in Teacher Training Colleges, in informal educational classes may learn to take a pride in African agriculture and to realize its strategic importance. "But we have been taken too literally. We do not suggest that all pupils should become farm labourers. We want the African countryside to develop in much the same way as the English; a community that depends on the land; not only the farmers and those directly employed in agriculture, but also those who live by supplying goods and services to farmers—professional and commercial men and so on. We want a healthy rural community life to balance the industrial community life."

But that cannot be realized till educated men are seized of the importance of agriculture; in other words till education is acclimatized, and rooted in the soil of Africa.

"Transplantation is mutation," it has been said, but this has not always been realised as applicable to education. There is a balance to be redressed, and the literal interpretation of the question "Is education rooted in the soil?" is a salutary reminder of that fact.

4. Spiritual Roots

Now we must thrust upon the attention of posterity what is perhaps the most distinctive characteristic of the Cambridge Conference and the reports on which it was based—their deep concern with the question, "Is education rooted in the *soul* of Africa?"

In 1925 the Secretary of State's Advisory Committee on Education insisted on the value of a religious basis for educational work. In words which have served as a charter of religious education ever since, they laid it down that: "Since contact with civilization, and even education itself, must necessarily tend to weaken tribal authority and the sanctions of existing beliefs, and in view of the all-prevailing belief in the supernatural which affects the whole life of the African, the greatest importance must be attached to religious teaching and moral instruction. Both in schools and in training colleges they should be accorded an equal standing with secular subjects." A committee appointed in 1940 by the then Governor of Uganda reported to the same effect though more emphatically Christian: "The Government recognizes more forcibly than ever that Western civilization ought to be built on the profoundly Christian basis and tradition which the Mission school is particularly fitted to provide; the highest public interest demands the inculcation of Christian values."

That is all very well for official bodies, but could it be expected that this policy would be endorsed in 1952 by a company so comprehensively and unofficially composed as the Cambridge Conference in which moreover those in any way formally representative of churches and missions were in a minority? Would it not inevitably succumb to moral platitude or humanitarian utopianism?

The Conference noted as one of the most impressive points of correspondence between the reports of the Western and Eastern Study Groups their common emphasis on the building up of moral leadership. They quote in full the following paragraph as an expression of their own convictions: " . . . The one who holds, whether by outward profession or by an inward and inarticulate knowing, that moral integrity, intellectual honesty, respect for persons, compassion and courage are good in themselves and that their goodness is not contingent on circumstances of time or place—the one who holds these things firmly and discovers the way to express them in action will be a good neighbour, a good teacher, parent or citizen, and a good leader among his people."

A few more quotations will show that this recognition of education's responsibility to meet a moral need, to inspire moral leadership and to develop character is no isolated or conventional obeisance to virtue.

Speaking of the example that one African can give to his fellows:

"A man who in any station of life is an upright man, fair and just in his dealing, kindly and considerate to his neighbours, is a living example of the good. We come to know the good less by any process of rational thinking than by acquaintance with the good. The moral progress of any people depends partly upon the vision and vigour of its prophets, but more upon the example of those men and women who by reason of consistent and faithful lives are judged worthy by their fellows."

*   *   *   *   *

"The exercise of character involves the ability to see the variety of action that is possible in a given concrete situation, the moral sensitivity to assess the nature of the consequences of each line of action, and the will to choose that which will best subserve the good. . . . Training of character is no easy business that can be accomplished in one step. . . . It must not stop at the establishment of rules, or sooner or later a man will fail to do right either because he finds himself in a situation not covered by the rules or because the sanction of the rules has grown weak."

*   *   *   *   *

"Two important elements in the exercise of character are discernment and judgment, and these are gifts which can be developed only by facing the actual circumstances of life in a given situation."

*   *   *   *   *

"Education will fail in its object if it does not inculcate a respect for truth. Wherever the old and new are as intermixed as they are in Africa it is particularly difficult to distinguish the true from the false. There is always the temptation to assume that the new is necessarily true and the old false, or the reverse. The development of this ability to distinguish the true from the false must be a fundamental aim of education."

*   *   *   *   *

"If the chief aim of education is the development of character the teacher should himself be a man of character. He should have the opportunity by participation in the corporate life of a college or otherwise for the kind of education which assists personal development and the growth of character."

* * * * *

"The next step in the inculcation of a new moral code is the substitution of active for passive morality by the strengthening of community life. In a school where community life is strong, moral habits grow strong until they become part of the personality."

* * * * *

"Education must seek to draw out all that is best in every man and woman, and has the threefold duty of preparing men and women to be good workers, to be good citizens, and to develop the spiritual insight with which God has blessed them."

* * * * *

The last words of the last quotation strike a note which is sounded again and again with the solemn reiteration of a tenor bell. "Any moral code worthy of the name must rest on the spiritual guidance that comes from deep and sincere religious belief. As Christians we naturally look to Christianity for our guidance, but we appreciate that the Muslim religion provides such guidance to many good men and women whose lives are examples to others. In the matter of religious belief we think that where governments have taken up a position of neutrality this attitude should no longer continue. A public statement on a belief in the necessity of a spiritual basis to education would give encouragement and strength to those already at work and provide the inspiration for future development."

"In connexion with our deep-rooted belief that religion must be the basis of education, we have considered the importance of the school chapel or place of worship. Governments have been very reluctant to contribute financially towards building chapels in schools managed from public funds, and governors and governments have urged that an assembly hall or classroom can be used as a chapel temporarily. We disagree with this assumption, believing as we do that the influence of a place of worship built and used only for that purpose will be profound."

Each of the five Groups into which the Conference broke up for discussion has something to say on this subject of religion.

Group A: "We accepted unanimously that secular education is not enough, and our deliberations presuppose an education with a religious basis and a spiritual doctrine of human nature and destiny. Without the formal association of religious bodies with the established secular forms of government, there can be no effectual guarantee of the type of education we presuppose."

Group B: "In order that a genuinely religious basis may be assured both for formal education and for youth work we hope that the Churches will devote more attention to urban communities and their peculiar problems."

Group C insists that: "Training College staff should be of such a high moral character as will fit them to exercise a sound influence upon their students, and that while they do not wish candidates to be subjected to a doctrinal test the high moral character they desire to see will be the manifestation of a convinced religious faith."

Group D: "Moral standards stem from and can neither be accepted nor taught without a basis of belief. Belief if it is to be effective must be positively and firmly held. . . . To teach about religion is not enough. It must be lived out in the whole life of the school community. The atmosphere of a school is determined by what the teachers are."

Group E pleads for more help from the Churches in its sphere of Adult Education.

Religion in education has Muslim as well as Christian champions. "There are in British Tropical Africa," they report, "many millions of Muslims who would be prejudiced against education if no adequate provisions were made in the educational system for religious instruction."

Translated into terms of policy these convictions appear to dictate that Native Authority and Local Education Authority schools "should have a religious basis. In any legislation in regard to schools not owned or managed by missions consideration should be given to introducing provisions which indicate the value of corporate worship and religious instruction, possibly in accordance with an agreed syllabus, special provision being made in respect of the children of Muslims."

D

Chapter Five

EDUCATIONAL LADDERS

DESCENDING from the sublime to the pedestrian, we must now sketch in some details of the educational system within the limitations of which the ideals outlined in our last chapter must be applied in practice. This system is sometimes described as a pyramid resting on a broad foundation of popular education, and tapering as it rises through middle and secondary levels to a small university apex. It has also been likened to a tree which only spreads out its branches and bears fruit after the sap has risen straight up within a narrow trunk to its full height.

The first metaphor is inspired by and inspires enthusiasm for broadening the base, even to the detriment of the higher levels of education. The second derives from the conviction that the education of the masses is not the root but the final fruit and deprecates impatience to gather the educational fruit till the tree has had time to grow: the education of the many is only made possible by the prolonged study and acquired learning of the few.

Pressed to their logical conclusions these metaphors would lead to sharply divergent policies. Exclusive adoption of either —the slowing down of primary school expansion in the interests of higher education, or the denial of higher education to the African in the interests of the elementary—would provoke lively, even violent, reactions. As mutual correctives both are valuable.

So much of *African Education* is devoted to the lower levels and so little to the apex that it might appear that its authors are wedded to the pyramidal conception; but there is nothing in this derogatory to the dignity of Higher Education.*

* See page 102 ff.

It is a recognition of the recent work of the Elliott and Asquith Commissions which covered that ground so adequately, leaving our present enquirers free to concentrate on the first twelve years of an educational career. A spear, it is recognised, will not be effective if it is all shaft or all blade. A blade of the finest metal, tempered and sharpened it must have, but it must be proportioned to a shaft massive enough to drive it home. In its discussions of the first twelve years of an educational career the Cambridge Conference was consciously placing its emphasis on the building of the new Africa—an Africa which needs an intelligent rank and file; which needs an enlightened teaching profession; which needs a source from which to supply its own Civil Service, its administrators and professional men, its clergy and ministers, its historians, and scientists, to whom nothing must be denied that will give full opportunity for the development of their gifts.

Educational Scaffolding

It will be in keeping with this Building-the-New-Africa ideal if we picture education as the scaffolding which makes that building possible; though this, like all impersonal metaphors, must not be pressed too far when applied to the sphere of personal relationships. Each stage of the scaffolding gives access to one storey of the building, where there is essential work to be done; each storey is linked to the one above by a ladder, each ladder reaching a platform which can serve either as destination for those whose lot is cast on that landing, or as stepping-off place for those destined to ascend to higher floors.

This figure could be worked out more tidily if all the architects and masons employed could agree on a common terminology, as well as on the spacing of the platforms and the consequent height of the ladders. Those working on the West wall do not, for example, mean the same thing as those on the East when they use such terms as "intermediate" or "middle" schools; while one side may be designing three platforms where the other is content with two. The figure 12 is obviously susceptible of division into 4 plus 4 plus 4 or 6 plus 6; six primary years and six secondary, or four primary, four middle, four secondary; or 6 may be split into 4 plus 2. These are highly technical questions not likely to be found interesting 500 years hence. The controversy does not affect the symmetry of the building as much as might be expected; "it does not affect the total length of school life but its organization into cycles of study." We may leave it to the expert, concentrating our attention on principles and problems common to all.

"On the objectives of educational policy we (The Cambridge Conference) are in complete agreement. We find their source in the desire of Africans that their countries (note the plural) should play a worthy part among the nations of the world, in the intellectual no less than in the economic sphere, developing their own cultural contribution to the common heritage of mankind." "The differing circumstances of the various territories must produce at any given time varying answers to the problems of school organisation, and work out their own solutions."

1. The Criterion of Advance

The first problem is "wastage," and the first principle is that a child setting foot on the bottom rung of any ladder must be induced to scale the whole ladder till it reaches the platform that belongs to it. While that applies to all ladders it is the first that offers the most acute difficulty. "Education targets have usually been thought of in terms of an increase in the total number of children at school or the total number of schools. A more important measure of advance is the percentage of an age-group who complete a cycle of studies, and not the number who begin it but fall by the way. What is greatly needed is more primary school-leavers, more middle school-leavers, more secondary school-leavers who have completed the full course. This should be the index of advance and all targets should be expressed in terms of the percentage of an age-group completing primary or middle or secondary school courses." Casualties haunt the educational mind of Africa, especially East and Central Africa, not without cause. In one territory the number of children in the lowest four classes in one given year were in the proportion of 40:23:10:5. All territories have a long way to go before they achieve the modest target suggested, namely 50% of the age-group scaling to the top of ladder 1, (a 4-year primary course), 10% scaling ladder 2, (a 4-year middle course) and 2% ladder 3, (a 4-year secondary course).

Casualties on this scale discount very largely the value of the whole educational system, and "involve an immense waste of money, and what is more important of good human material. If we accept the view of 75% of our witnesses the average child cannot attain to literacy in less than 4 years and if a child does not get literacy he gets nothing: all the money spent on educating a child who does not stay the 4 years course is wasted as completely as if it had been burned, while there is the waste of human material to be added to the debit side of the account. In territories where there is not enough money available to educate more than a fraction of the children it is clear that a high proportion of the money that *is* being spent is being completely wasted." "Wastage is also a factor to be reckoned with in post-primary schools, particularly in the case of girls many of whom leave to get married before they complete a middle or secondary course: the loss of teaching power and of school places is immense."

We have noted in an earlier chapter some of the causes of truancy. Here we are concerned with the remedies proposed. Some of these are long-term prescriptions and depend for their validity on the evolution of African society and social custom. Some are beyond the competence of teachers to effect for themselves. The limitation of all classes to a reasonable number is one such: Northern Rhodesia has found by experiment that classes of 35 produce higher numbers of those completing the course than did classes of 50. Another is the elimination of a custom, which is strongly deprecated as encouraging wastage, of imposing an ascending scale of fees for each rung of the ladder.

But among the remedies fourteen in number which the Conference advocated there are some which a headmaster and his staff could apply. They could establish closer relations with parents, enlisting their active co-operation in school affairs. The interest of chiefs and other influential Africans could be won. No one but the teaching staff can apply the first remedy proposed, "Lively teaching and attractive schools," to counteract the depressing effect of boredom, drabness and mystification as to what it is all about. They can regulate admissions so that the age of children entering the school, and the age-range of the classes offer a reasonable chance of pupils completing the course. Holidays can be arranged to coincide with the main agricultural seasons—planting, weeding, bird-scaring, reaping. Automatic promotion is also recommended; provided that attendance has been regular no child should normally be required to stay in the same class for a second year. This is an antidote to undue retardation which aggravates wastage.

2. Self-contained Courses

A second principle affirmed with some unanimity is that each ladder must provide an experience complete in itself, self-contained and worthwhile for those who are unlikely to climb higher beyond the next landing. The problem besets primary education in particular, though not confined to the first course, for large numbers are involved. The Western Group points out that primary education has two functions to perform. It must provide a satisfying course for the great majority whose schooling ends at or before the end of the primary stage. It must also provide a satisfactory grounding for the few who go on to a secondary education. In the bigger towns and in some districts, so insistent is the demand for secondary education that this second function has assumed in the eyes of teachers and public an importance out of all proportion to the very small number who do in fact climb further; the minor role has come to overshadow the major. Many schools have been on the whole "less unsuccessful in preparing the few for secondary schools than in preparing the many for life. No other result can reasonably be expected from schools which, ignoring time and distance, attempt to model themselves in organisation and curriculum on the English elementary school of forty years ago!" Hence the stern insistence on self-contained courses.

First Ladder

Ladder 1, for example, should give a child arriving at the first platform entry to a storey in the New Africa Building where he would find himself or herself at home in the company of literates, able to read and write his own language, having acquired sound standards of conduct, and some understanding of the community and the individual's place in the community; he or she should have acquired skill of hand sufficient to stimulate a recognition of the value of manual work, and should have developed a lively curiosity about the environment and the world outside. The Conference noted and welcomed the close agreement of the two Study Groups and of its five working-parties, that character and "the building up of leadership" were of overwhelming importance.

Second Ladder

For those who are lucky enough to be among the 25% of primary school leavers qualified to mount higher, ladder 2 should offer an attractive variety of new experiences and disciplines that will qualify them on arrival at platform 2 to join the company "of resourceful and intelligent Africans who are literate in English, and have had a sound practical and general education in a school where the key-note has been service of the community."

"The middle schools therefore occupy a most crucial position in relation to education expansion. Their pupils can help to produce the wealth, and must produce the teachers necessary before any further expansion is possible in primary education. They must also be numerous enough to provide sufficient able candidates to go forward to secondary education."

"The expansion of middle schools must be given the first priority. Their curriculum should be a carefully integrated blend of the theoretical and the practical, so devised that theoretical work rises always from practical and concrete beginnings: agriculture and animal husbandry associated with theoretical work in biology, commercial studies associated both with language and mathematics, building and machine construction associated with mathematics, and for girls the household arts. The technical and scientific elements in this course would be balanced by a course called social studies, in which the study of current affairs local and universal would be an introduction to history, geography and civics."

It is on arrival at the second platform that the majority will find their way into vocational halls which open off the second storey of the building, teacher training and nurse training institutions and their equivalent for other walks of life.

Third Ladder

Those who are ambitious to reach a yet higher school certificate platform will have to jostle with a crowd of competitors scrambling for a place on the next ladder, for secondary schools are scarce and likely to remain so till Africa has had time to multiply her teachers of quality. For the time being secondary education cannot get on without expatriate reinforcements, and they are expensive. Buildings also are needed and they too are expensive. A high standard has been set and there are secondary school buildings in Africa that would be the envy of their opposite numbers in England.

There are also questions of major policy to be decided before Africa can go forward confidently with a secondary education programme of the magnitude required. There is for example the conflict between size and number: "From the educational point of view a smaller number of larger schools is likely to prove more efficient than a larger number of smaller schools."

"One of the biggest dangers threatening the healthy growth of education on the West Coast is that the demand for secondary education will be met by the opening of schools which have neither the staff nor the buildings which are essential if the pupils are to receive a proper secondary education. In both these matters the laying down and enforcing of sound minimum standards is essential. To lay down standards which are not always enforced, and which, even if they were, are so low as to give a cloak of rectitude to schools the very existence of which is in fact a scandal, may produce a temporary slackening of political pressure but must produce ultimate educational disaster."

3. Two-fold Parting of the Ways

Our successful competitor will now find himself, perhaps for the first time, faced with the necessity of choosing between alternatives. First he must choose between two types of secondary school, the grammar school and the technical school. His future career begins to loom and his aptitudes to reveal themselves, and he must make his decision accordingly.

THE FIRST CHOICE: GRAMMAR OR TECHNICAL?

a. Grammar Schools

It is against the secondary grammar school that the charge of bookishness is most frequently levelled. "One of the complaints is that the curriculum is both bookish and useless, too little related to the life of the pupils outside the classroom, and useless as a preparation for the lives they will lead after they leave school. There is some truth in this but the remedy lies as much in changing the treatment of subjects already given a place in the curriculum as in introducing subjects at present lacking." "The danger that besets all secondary schools in Africa is that an academic education will estrange pupils from the realities of African life. At every secondary school there should be some well-managed agricultural work linked intelligently to some part of the academic work of the school, in order that the future leader of African life should be aware of the paramount importance of agriculture and of the dignity of manual tasks."

The proposed treatment of History as a subject is an indication of the desired approach to academic subjects. "There are two essentials. First that the African should grasp the essence of European historical values, as Europeans for generations absorbed classical historical values. Only if the leaders of African life have been inspired by European cultural values will they be able to adapt these to African needs, and be saved from either a slavish imitation of European civilisation or an unbalanced reaction against it. The second essential is that Africans should know sufficient of the recent history of Africa to understand and develop their own economic, political, social and constitutional life."

b. Technical Schools

Technical secondary education, still at an early stage, and too young to be ranked as a co-equal with the secondary grammar school, is exposed to the opposite criticism, that it is not academic enough. But it is intended that the secondary technical school should provide a general education broadly comparable in quality with that given in the grammar school, while paying more attention to the appropriate science and to practical work in wood and metal and to agriculture. "Perhaps even more than in Europe successful technical education can only be given to the African on the basis of a good general education. Attempts have been made to produce skilled craftsmen quickly in response to clamant demands from governments and industry, and most of them have failed. Anybody can be shown how to use tools, and to work in gangs under supervision, but the skilled craftsman needs to be able to tackle a job with no more than a general indication of what is required, and to see it through: he must be able to read a blue-print, and a technical drawing; he must know what material and what type of construction are appropriate, and be able to hold his own in face of intense competition from Indian craftsmen."

THE SECOND ALTERNATIVE: BOARDING SCHOOLS OR DAY SCHOOLS?

The second choice is between day schools and boarding schools. If our candidate in his perplexity sought the advice of the Cambridge Conference there is little doubt what form that would take. The boarding school is favoured partly on grounds of expediency, in spite of its expense, "for it will be many years before any but the largest towns can find enough secondary day pupils to fill a school of reasonable size, and in the rural areas it is very doubtful if there can be any alternative to the boarding school for secondary students. A smaller number of larger schools would be more efficient educationally than the converse." Our candidate therefore may be spared the necessity of making a choice for the issue will be decided for him.

But the case for boarding schools does not rest on expediency alone. "In the social conditions prevailing in the West African territories there can be no doubt of the immense benefit which the vast majority of pupils derive from the stable living and working conditions of a good boarding school. Furthermore they can by providing good material conditions and setting good social standards, do much to spread the knowledge of healthy living far beyond their own walls. It would indeed be hard to exaggerate the importance of the part that boarding education, even on its present small scale, has played in social development, or the opportunities which await its extension." The Conference endorsed this view. "Boarding schools have positive advantages in the opportunities they offer for character-training, for raising standards of living, and for bringing together pupils from different communities." The last point deserves stressing: in a plural society—and it must be remembered that African society in addition to very diverse African elements comprises also Asian and European elements—it means much for the consolidation and future unity of the country if during their formative years her citizens have known what it is to live in a community in which sectional loyalties are transcended in a common loyalty, where merit and personality alone count, where school friendships are formed that last through life, and the fundamental lesson is learnt—to respect (not to resent) the otherness of other men.

For developing girls' education boarding schools are held to be indispensable; very few places could support a girls' day secondary school, and parents are reluctant to send their daughters to a mixed school. The Cambridge Conference was not against co-education even though its time has not yet come for adoption as a general policy. "Our opinion in general is that co-education can play a vital part in girls' education, particularly in giving at least to the more promising girls assurance and confidence. Where this is impossible a close relationship between girls' and boys' schools in social activities, in exchange of staff and sharing school facilities can be valuable."

For this reason the idea must be outgrown that girls' boarding institutions should "be buried in some remote spot to isolate both school and staff from disturbing influences: it puts the girls in social quarantine in term-time, ignoring the different situation in their holidays, and isolating them from an environment which they should be studying at first hand; it makes an unnatural and difficult setting for staff."

"There is a growing conviction among responsible Africans

that the future of their people depends upon the existence of a sound proportion of educated women."

"There is a widespread and sincere recognition of the need to extend qualitatively and quantitatively educational facilities for women and girls."

"Very little has yet been done to explore the possibilities of careers for girls apart from teaching and nursing. But that other careers are now regarded as possible for African girls marks the beginning of a change in the whole conception of the place of women and girls in African society."

4. Tests

African education is obviously likely to remain heavily selective for many years to come. How is the selecting to be done? Who or what is to decide whether and when a child is to move on from rung to rung, and from ladder to ladder? Who is to judge which of 14,000 candidates for secondary education are to fill the 800 places available?

"All the children in West coast schools are far more frequently and persistently examined than is desirable. The average child may well spend something like a third of his school life being examined or revising for examinations. Many African teachers would probably be shocked at the suggestion that examinations were not a good thing in themselves. Many of the examinations which now clutter the educational system have lost any educational justification they may once have had, and are retained in spite of their pernicious effects because they are a convenient peg on which Governments, and consequently other employers, may hang their jobs."

Africa is by no means the only country in which examinations are the subject of much heart-searching; they provoke universal scrutiny. But the analogy between Africa and other countries may be misleading, for Africa has her own special problems. We are told for example that the use of intelligence tests in Africa is attended with special difficulties. "We do not consider it advisable to import into Africa tests used in England or to place reliance on them before they have been tried and standardized in Africa; they should evolve in their proper educational climate, and this process will be slow." The Institute of Education at Makerere has begun constructive research in intelligence testing as applied to East Africa.

Again the grievance against examination pressure has its special African expression. "The pressure of examinations in secondary schools is very largely responsible for the attitude of mind which regards practical work in agriculture as a waste of time that should be used for examination cramming. The reform of the system might do much negatively to improve the attitude of educated Africans towards agriculture and practical work."

The Cambridge report inaugurates a resistance movement against "an intolerable tyranny." There are four points of attack:

i. *Internal primary school examinations*, which are generally terminal and are often reinforced by monthly, fortnightly, or even weekly tests.

ii. *Rung to rung examinations* for certificates intended to mark the reaching of a certain standard.

"A reduction in the number of these internal and standard examinations is obviously desirable, but it is equally desirable to change the character of those which are retained. At present they are generally difficult in the sense that they demand the maximum of factual knowledge, and easy in the sense that they do not demand any real understanding of that knowledge. They tend to be tests of memory rather than of thinking."

The Eastern Study Group's investigation into the method by which children pass through the first four standards "revealed a complicated system of annual tests and examinations on which promotions depend. The ability and potentiality of the youngest age-groups cannot and should not be assessed quantitively, and it should be possible on the class teacher's recommendation for all children to have a clear run through the first four years.

iii. *Ladder to ladder examinations*, of which the most formidable is that for selection for secondary grammar schools.

These too come in for harsh criticism: "They appear to be

based on the entirely fallacious assumption that the harder the questions the greater the selective power of the examination is likely to be. The papers are based on the principle of hard questions and lenient marking, and emphasize attainment rather than ability. No attempt is made to obtain the advice of primary school teachers as to their suitability. The effectiveness or futility of any part of the examination or indeed of the whole of it remains hidden through the apparent absence of any post-mortem."

"The selective examination for middle schools should be as slight as is consistent with its purpose in order not to distort the curriculum of the primary school, and should be designed not to test the efficiency of primary school education but potential ability for middle school education."

The Conference considered that there are three main ways in which information about each pupil can be obtained, and that ideally all three should be used.

    a. From the primary school records: these should be not so much factual records of attainment but something which will provide some clue to the pupil's abilities. Teachers in training should be well taught about the art of assessment.

    b. Interview with the candidate, carried out by a small committee composed of school staff and one or two persons from outside, remaining the same throughout to maintain a consistent standard.

    c. A written examination of some sort, sufficient to provide some objective element in selection.

    iv. *External examinations.* "At present the only examination of this kind is that provided by the Cambridge Examining Body. The examination has been adapted to the needs of African pupils in many ways, but it is considered doubtful whether its influence on the African secondary school curriculum is now wholly good. Even the mathematical papers are still impregnated with an English background and include problems on 'men and bathtaps' or 'trains and tunnels.' Its English papers are heavy with grammar and 19th-century literature, while other subjects have been only partially adapted from the normal syllabus of an English school, instead of being thought out wholly with the needs of Africa in mind."

Nevertheless the Conference concluded that "external examinations were not undesirable in themselves, if only teachers and pupils did not allow them to colour their outlook unduly. The Cambridge Examination Syndicate has proved itself to be always willing to consider sympathetically any suggestion for the revision of syllabus. Moreover, examining is a matter for experts, and the Cambridge examination is particularly valuable because of its consistency in maintaining and developing good standards in African education."

Chapter Six

EDUCATIONAL PARTNERS

POSTERITY wanted to know what kind of schools were in existence in the Africa of 1952, and we have tried to describe for their benefit the educational system as articulated by so representative a body as the Cambridge Conference. The further questions arose (page 12): Were there educational authorities responsible for the provision, maintenance and expansion of the system? In particular were governments alive to their responsibilities in the matter? General responsibility for African education is, as we have seen, shared out between parents, teachers, clergy and ministers, inspectors, examiners, teacher-trainers, and the whole company of builders of the new Africa. But our questioners want to know upon whose shoulders rests responsibility for major decisions on matters of high policy and for implementing them.

The partners in this kind of responsibility may be defined as two, the official and unofficial, but the former subdivides into central official and local official, and we must therefore deal with the relations between three partners—the Central Government, Local Government, and what are called Voluntary Agencies. It will be least invidious if we take them in chronological order—in the order in which they put in an appearance on the African educational field, and give precedence to the unofficial agencies.

1. The Unofficial Partner

Both Study Groups agree, as any historian must, that the Church began the work of African education. As the Eastern Group says, "It is the historical role of the Churches to be the trail-blazers in adventures that affect the well-being of people whether in education, health or the welfare of the young, the

64

old, or the handicapped. The Churches have made the initial experiments, have learnt how to bring success out of failure, and have handed over to Governments their achievements to develop. The story of voluntary agencies in these territories has not deviated much from this pattern, and African and European alike know and willingly acknowledge how much is owed to the efforts of the voluntary agencies in the days before administrations developed the positive policy now pursued."

Similarly the Western Group: "Long before it became a recognized responsibility of Government to make provision for education schools were established and carried on by Churches and by devoted men and women." This confirms the judgment of the De la Warr Commission on Higher Education in East Africa, 1937, and the Elliott Commission on Higher Education in West Africa, 1945.

The question remains whether the task of the unofficial partner is ended, and if not what is to be the relation between unofficial and official. It would not be surprising if anything so nearly approaching a monopoly as the Churches enjoyed for so long—in some countries 80 to 90% of the educational work—aroused some of the resentment which monopolies incur even when not run for profit. It seems unfair that they got such a good start. Murmurs of "vested interests" might even be heard. It would not be surprsing if "mission" education for a newer generation smelt of days far remote when the patriarchal pioneer exercised paternal dominion; when policy was controlled not in Africa but in London or Rome, when individualism held sway, and no one thought in terms of an African nation. Ulterior motive might be suspected. The word "proselytist" makes a good hiss. Sectarian aggrandisement may have taken precedence of educational sincerity? Power casts its spell on the holiest men and women.

But putting this question does not necessarily imply adverse criticism: the facts suggest it. How can missions expect to keep pace with so rapid an expansion of such an increasingly expensive education? Have they the man-power? Can they staff all these training colleges and secondary schools? Can they maintain management with efficient administration and accountancy? Had they not better resign in favour of the official

E

partner, rather than cumber the ground with schools lower in standard than others owing to straitened resources?

That the Study Groups had come across misunderstandings and misrepresentations is clear from the pains they take to counteract them.

> "The attitude of the impartial educationalist on the relation of the educational work of religious bodies to that of the state system is likely to be utterly different according to whether he judges that the motive of the religious body is a desire to gain some sectional advantage or derives from a sense of religious duty to make a characteristic contribution to a common cause, in the belief that the spread of enlightenment is the surest means of leading people to a knowledge of the truth. There are uncomfortable facts which lend colour to the first alternative, such as the mal-distribution of schools and continued failure to co-operate when co-operation has become a manifest educational necessity, but the missions of the West Coast are entitled to claim in their record that the second motive has far outweighed the first."

The Eastern Group reports that representatives of African bodies in giving evidence have quite often referred to "their" schools and "ours" as defining the difference between mission schools and those provided by African local authorities. But the distinction was disallowed by the Conference. "Many voluntary agency schools in Africa are run by trusts and committees composed entirely of Africans. Further, Christianity has made such progress in Africa that in many places there are self-governing Churches." Several speakers stressed the fact that voluntary agencies denominational as well as secular were often just as African in composition and in feeling as some local government authorities themselves. One speaker testified that "voluntary agencies far from regarding each other as rivals work together in close collaboration. It would be just as wrong to imagine that they are controlled by Europeans. They have set up compact bodies of control, many of which are almost wholly composed of African members. There is a great deal of excellent African leadership available in these bodies." Another speaker said that: "Voluntary agency schools can be just as much people's schools as those which are run by a local authority. The agency I represent does not think in terms of a mission, but of the diocesan education council; this is a democratic body of three missionaries and over forty African clergy and laity."

No edict went forth from the Conference to dissolve partnership with the unofficial partner. On purely educational grounds their schools were commended "as educational associations of great value which the country could ill afford to lose : they attract teachers of quality who might not be attracted to service in other schools; by reason of their religious foundations many such schools have special opportunities to promote moral education and character-building." "Within any educational system diversity of organization may be an advantage in that it gives wider opportunities for experiment and development." One African teacher said that when his country became self-governing it would still need the services of the voluntary agencies : he agreed that they should continue not merely to use their educational buildings, but to be properly represented on the governing bodies of schools. No voice was raised to disagree with him.

There is indeed one direction in which it is thought that the Churches might well extend their work—"It is a curious thing that the Churches generally play so small a part in adult education work. This is curious because loss of literacy is liable to lead to loss of religion, and this also seems to be work peculiarly suited to the genius of a voluntary and religious society."

The Conference decisively rejected any suggestion that the day of the unofficial partner was passing and that it might "be simpler and more effective to have within each territory or region one uniform comprehensive school system." If there are any totalitarians left in the 25th century there is little doubt what their answer will be; they will say that everything has gone wrong in African education between then and now because the 20th century was too muddled over the beauties of diversity to institute a one-party, monolithic educational system.

These are questions to which answers applicable to the varying circumstances of different parts of Africa must be found." The danger lies in half-hearted answers. A voluntary agency by its name implies an offer of help beyond what could be demanded as an obligation. "If this offer is accepted with West African open-heartedness much good may come of it in the years ahead. If it is accepted reluctantly and with many reservations and restrictions the kernel of the voluntary spirit may shrivel within its husk. There may still be schools of this type but they will be less effective than they might have been if the sun of due acknowledgment had sometimes shone."

2. *The Central Official Partner*

The official partner can use the power of coercion, the unofficial only the power of persuasion. The former can (up to a point) rely on compulsory taxation, the latter mainly on voluntary offerings: the former covers the whole state, the latter only its special sphere of influence. But the motives of both alike are suspected by the suspicious. The unofficial "is primarily interested in religion not in education." The official "is primarily interested in order not in education." Both look on education as cement guaranteeing them perpetuity, and consolidating society, be it Church or State. When the self-interested motive and the disinterested converge on a single objective it is congenial to the cynic to call the second mere camouflage for the first.

The anti-totalitarian (if we may assume his survival into the 25th century) must be allowed his turn. "The Group began by laying it down that there comes a time in the development of a nation and of its educational system when the nation assumes responsibility for the control of education, and it is clear that it was thought that the time had already arrived in some parts of Africa." Does not this go much further, our questioner asks, than for example the words of Sir Michael Sadler, so often quoted on your day? As chairman of a Calcutta University Commission in 1920 he argued that "Education is a factor too important in national life for the state to abrogate its responsibilities in regard to it," but he went on to say it was "too intimately connected with family life and with private conviction to be entrusted to governmental management alone."

Everything has gone wrong in African education between then and now, the anti-totalitarian will say, because in 1952 you allowed the state to get away with the first half of the dictum and to suppress the second. Your capitulation to the fashionable charm of the so-called omnicompetent state has a lot to answer for. Your identification with government was all very well when all was going smoothly, but as soon as issues arose stirring the very depths of African emotion, or presenting a moral challenge on which unofficial public opinion should be vocal, where were you then? You became too indistinguishable from the official to escape whatever censure or resistance official policy might incur. And what about your calling your teachers civil servants? How could they be expected to show originality or maintain their integrity? You muzzled them. Any lapse from ideological orthodoxy within the classroom or outside would be dangerous thinking, and fatal to their careers. They were bound to be at the mercy of every new education-department bureaucrat, and at the whim of every officious inspector.

There are many indications in *African Education* that our anti-totalitarian was not the first to think of these issues; they had not been unnoticed five hundred years before. As for inspectors: "Inspection is so specialised and exacting a function that it can only be carried out by highly qualified officers. who are able to devote their full time to it, but by inspection we mean an objective assessment of standards attained, and not the supervision by which those standards are attained. Inspection should be the function of the central authority only, but this role while necessary in present circumstances should not be regarded as a permanent feature of the educational system."

This final qualification would probably have to be dinned into the ears of this obstreperous anti-totalitarian many times before he arrived at the intention in the minds of the 20th century. He must make due allowance for the youth of the African educational system. There is a British tradition that in educational matters as much as possible should be left to the judgment of educators, as much as possible deputed and decentralised. Hence the ideal put before the Conference took the shape of a commonwealth of free educational societies not an educational empire or central dictatorship: recent British experience of a bi-partisan educational policy had pointed the benefit of rescuing education from party politics. But it would be agreed that in the earlier stages or when major changes are being inaugurated governments may have to decide more themselves, and take the initiative as in 1902 in Great Britain, and in Africa during recent decades. It would have been a bad look-out for Africa if governments had not taken a strong educational initiative; education cannot do without their authority co-terminous with national boundaries, and their resources.

Teachers in Public Life

The Conference gave much time to the discussion of the teacher in public life and its attitude may be found reassuring both for itself and as symptomatic of a general attitude to the role of Government in education.

> "Teachers in Africa form such a large proportion of the small body of educated citizens that their help is needed in public affairs: this public responsibility was so great that even the pupils' interests might properly be, to a limited extent, set aside to enable the teacher to carry out his responsibility as a citizen. A teacher should be encouraged to play his part in local government affairs as a member of a local authority, being given a reasonable amount of leave for the purpose."

> Again: "We think that local and national politics need the contribution which educated men and women like teachers can make. We appreciate that in times past, when 'politics' often meant merely opposition to the Government it would have been embarrassing to the Government to have civil servants openly opposing the policy they were officially supposed to carry out. But we feel that nowadays any disadvantage of having a teacher known to be a partisan will be outweighed by the advantage of having his services available in public life. We think that all teachers should be encouraged to take part in public affairs."

Membership of the central legislature presents more difficulty; a teacher could not combine that with school work, but it is recommended that he should be given "leave without pay to enable him to enter the legislature and that provision should be made for him to resume his profession when he desires without loss of rights and privileges." There is no muzzling of teachers here, except in so far as every teacher worth his salt will keep a check on himself lest he unfairly thrust his own political convictions down the throat of his pupils, coercing or indoctrinating the growing mind; lest also he forfeit the goodwill and respect of parents who may dislike his views.

3. The Local Official Partner

A teacher who goes in for local politics may combine in his own person the Unofficial and the Official and should be a valuable bridge between them. He will be able to bring some specialist experience to the benefit of the local education authority. Where there is, as there must sometimes be, some want of harmony between the longer established unofficial agency and the rising official agency he will have the chance of being a reconciler. He will also find himself cheek by jowl with representatives of unofficial agencies other than his own, and again become a reconciler in the interdenominational rivalries which are noted as a blot on the educational landscape.

The development of Local Government and Local Education Authority has been one of the most striking features of recent African history, and will be described in the following chapter.

Here is an official partner with whom unofficial partners will have to live on more intimate and neighbourly terms than with a central official partner.

There has (as has been noted) been no exchanging of notices to terminate partnership. in spite of much necessary difference of opinion as to how satisfactory terms can be agreed upon. There is all the difference between partnership and the identification which our anti-totalitarian friend deplored. Identities are not merged. There is no over-riding of individuality. On the contrary each partner insists on the others feeling at perfect liberty to make their distinctive contribution, with confidence that all are watching each with genuine goodwill and an expectant understanding.

There is, as in all things worth doing, a large element of faith in this planning. There is no guarantee that all governments will see eye to eye with those who argue cogently that: "A department of education is in a sense a service department, engaged in producing trained personnel for all other departments. Any considerable increase in productivity demands intelligence and expert knowledge. Among the social services, therefore, expenditure on education ought to have the highest priority." Even if that were agreed there is no guarantee that governments will have financial resources at their command to implement plans for expansion.

Again so remarkable a recommendation as that which is called "our main recommendation" (on the provision of funds) cannot expect to command at once the approval of all official partners, and even some of the unofficial show some inclination to look a gift horse in the mouth. It runs as follows: "All schools within the approved framework should be treated alike; the cost, both capital and recurrent, of all approved schools managed by voluntary agencies should be met entirely from public funds, central and local. This seems implicit in the principle we have laid down that the dichotomy of 'state' and 'church' schools must be avoided at all costs. . . . We have considered the view that the churches should retain a financial stake, however small, but it does not seem to have weight."

The case for the Church school rests sufficiently upon "the acknowledged necessity for a religious basis for education." In the course of the debate doubts were expressed whether assistance from the State to the extent of 100% would not restrict freedom to give the education that parents desired. On the other hand the assurance was given that freedom of management and control would suffer no reduction. Moreover "The idea that a Church or religious body can so to speak buy the opportunity to make its special contribution to education by making an appropriate financial payment is an unfortunate legacy from English educational history. The only right to take part in educational effort is the ability to make a good contribution and a sense of duty under which to make it." As one African spokesman put it "The complexion of the governing body of a school should depend upon the *ethos* of the school, not upon finance."

There are many highly technical details involved in plans for partnership between official and unofficial which must be reserved for a chapter to themselves. It will probably be enough for the general reader to realize that whatever difference of opinion on details there might be, the Conference was completely united in its determination that African education must continue to be run in a harmonious partnership between the three partners, the central and local official partners and the unofficial partner. That spirit of partnership found embodiment in a company as heterogeneous as the Cambridge Conference, and the same forces which bred it there may be equally operative on an indefinitely extended stage. It was the magnitude of the educational enterprise which inspired a new perspective, and the discovery of a very large and important area of agreement.

Chapter Seven

LOCAL RELATIONSHIPS

FUTURE annalists will not be content to know that a triple partnership was designed in Cambridge five hundred years before between central official, local official and voluntary agencies. Blue prints are all very well, but will they work? The use of scaffolding and ladder imagery may well disguise the fact that education has to do with human beings and human nature. While the central official partner may be august and remote enough for its relations with local partners to survive without shocks, will the same be true of partners exposed to the daily rub of intimate contact? Was it not making unrealistic demands on human nature to expect perpetual harmony and mutual confidence in a situation bristling with occasions of friction, conflicting interests and suspicions deriving from past and present rivalries? Is either local partner sure enough of its ground to maintain its dignity and good humour, eschewing competition and cultivating the spirit of co-operation?

1. The Official Local Partner

i. Local Government Authorities in Africa

Local government in Africa is, it is true, very young. It is not very old in England in its present form, but there the soil enriched by the accumulated humus of generations of public-spirited and unpaid service was favourable. Africa has its own tradition of corporate responsibility, but twentieth-century conceptions of democratic local self-government could not claim direct descent from them, as being the natural evolution of African custom. None the less the records are likely to show, local government came to stay, and no government of an African Territory has quarrelled with the 1947 despatch which inaugurated a policy of devolving responsibility. It defined the intentions as:

A. To create machinery for developing local opinion and for converting that opinion into action, thus establishing a framework for economic social and political development in the area, and the foundations for political development in the territory as a whole.

B. To provide experience and training in the control of public affairs for the greatest possible number of people.

The general plan was "to devolve executive and financial responsibility as far as possible on to local government authorities, and to ensure that those authorities are representative of and responsible to the local communities.

"Decentralisation of authority is designed to bring the local population into closer and more active co-operation with government, to give them wider channels of expression and initiative and to unite the different elements of the population of an area for common action giving the progressive trained and educated elements a fair share of responsibility, and bringing them into harmonious co-operation with the traditional tribal leaders. . . . It is hoped to stimulate general initiative and energy, and thus mobilize local government for all-round progress."

Legislation implementing this policy has varied from territory to territory; the details are not relevant to our present subject. In six out of eleven territories, representing 35 out of 53 million inhabitants autonomous revenue-raising local authorities have been or are being set up. That they have not shirked their less pleasant duties is clear from a comparison between the revenue raised by local authorities at the beginning and end of a very short period:

		1947-48	1951-52
Kenya	. .	£500,100	£1,036,200
Tanganyika	.	£1,040,169	£1,534,447
Nigeria (W.)	.	£888,014	£1,456,604
Gold Coast .	.	£478,489	£1,976,951

Such efforts have been recognized by increased central grants, and by the provision of loan-raising powers to finance capital development.

ii. Local Education Authorities

So much it has been necessary to sketch in of the setting in which local education authorities do their work. In the United Kingdom the Local Education Authority for each County is the County Council acting through its Education Committee. In Africa there are diversities of administration between territories, and different degrees of approximation to the homogeneous British pattern. In one it is proposed that every District Council should set up an Education Committee of its own members, plus nominated experts: in another the Local Education Authority is an ad hoc committee for each area designed to give representation to all interested parties, including the Local Government Authority: in another the Local Government Authority has the right of appointing its representatives on the ad hoc committee. Similarly the powers of the Local Education Authorities and their relations to the central authority show variations, but whatever their precise constitutional status Local Education Authorities fit into the Local Government picture and carry responsibility for the local application of educational policy.

We must now turn back to Cambridge. We are given a summary of the responsibilities devolving upon Local Education Authorities, some of which they share with the Central Authority. Their plans, for example, must square with the latter's over-all development plan, particularly in all that concerns secondary grammar and technical schools and their curricula. Local Education Authorities must be prepared to accept Government audit, and demands for statistical returns, Government arbitration when interests conflict, and to some extent Government specifications, such as those regulating the acreage required for different schools. The establishment of a unified teaching service is recommended, involving a uniformity of salary scales, terms of service, registration and removal from the Register which only a central authority can effect. Inspection again is a function of central authority, but this is sharply distinguished from supervision, the former being confined to an objective assessment of standards attained, leaving Local Education Authorities responsible for supervision of the means by which those standards are or are not attained. Inspectors are not given any executive functions, but merely record their findings.

Within these limits there is a wide range of responsibilities confided to local authorities. Theirs is the initiative in establishing and siting new primary schools. They disburse all grants within the approved framework, which includes safeguards against preferential treatment of Local Education Authority as against Voluntary Agency schools. The planning, building, equipping, furnishing and maintenance of schools are local concerns, as are the posting and payment of registered teachers, and the granting of scholarships and bursaries at the primary level. "Informal education is vital to the proper operation of the formal school system, and must be very closely co-ordinated with it. It is bound to be rooted in the daily life of the people, and so must clearly be a special concern of the local authorities."

iii. Boards of Management

An authority may be local as distinct from central, and local in the sense that it can survey the educational needs of a locality, and yet fail to be local to the extent of being in personal touch with local problems and persons. Every school therefore must have its Board of Managers in day-to-day touch with its head, its teachers and its parents, its buildings and equipment. "It was on the subject of the fullest African participation in management that we were most happily and proudly unanimous. Each school or group of schools should have a board of Managers, with representatives of the Churches, African wherever possible, and of the local government body in appropriate proportions."

If in its provision of boards of management Cambridge owes much to English practice, it is Scottish precedent that has influenced the thinking of the Conference on the broader aspects of local education authorities, though conclusions drawn from English or Scottish precedents are suspect as having little validity in Africa, over against the bewildering diversity of conditions between territory, and even between different areas of the same territory. Moreover Britain possesses a system of universal compulsory education which Africa as yet lacks: it can rely on a teaching profession of maturity and experience "at a level of responsibility which would largely ensure the continuance of the essential work of the schools even if much of the administrative machinery were missing. Whereas in the United Kingdom the Central Government has no executive function in education, in Africa the central governments have many."

In looking ahead to the future of local education authorities the Conference accepts as axiomatic the real devolution of power and responsibility: local government must mean nothing less. "If Africans are to find adequate expression for their new hopes and aspirations, they must have opportunities to serve the public interests of their country in their immediate communities, and real service needs an element of responsibility. Participation in local affairs is at once a present service and a preparation for the larger services the future will require of them. History provides no formula by which peoples can arrive at full political maturity save along the hard road of steadily increasing executive responsibility."

iv. District Councils.

This basic assumption dictates the conclusion that the local education authorities should be integrated with the organ of local government, the District Council. The District Council as itself ultimately if not at once the Local Education Authority, should establish education committees, to whom it would delegate all educational functions except the approval of the annual estimates. "*Ad hoc* education authorities may be transition forms, but should not survive as the final pattern in a fully developed African system."

It may be wondered why there should be any tolerance of "transition forms". Is it consistent with its basic principle that the Conference commends the care with which the Eastern group defined four successive stages by which local education authorities would reach fullness of stature? Beginning as a nominated advisory body, they were the first to drop the "nominated" and become representative, secondly to drop the "advisory" and

become executive, before blossoming out as full-blown education committees to which the district councils would delegate all
functions relating to education. The Conference certainly took
the view that the "hard road of steadily increasing executive responsibility" could not be covered in seven-league boots, but
that, given efficient executive officers, progress could be swifter
to the executive stage than these four steps imply provided that
care be taken not to overload the new authorities with functions and responsibilities. While not going beyond the primary
stage, the Conference foresaw a further line of development,
"recording the opinion" that "these functions which are dis-
charged locally in respect of primary schools should as local
authorities grow in experience, efficiency and resources be dis-
charged similarly in respect of post-primary institutions serving
the area.

It may safely be inferred that the note of caution arises not
from any depreciation of the human element, but from lively
appreciation of complexities and perplexities inherent in local
government and not least in local education administration.
Education has a deceptive appearance of simplicity, so that
every Tom, Dick and Harry claims the right to be dogmatic
about it. It is an emotional subject exciting passionate advocacy
of rival policies. It affects intimate domestic life and affections
coming under the day-to-day scrutiny of every father and
mother. It sets District Councils a nice problem in priorities. Its
claims to a share of the local revenue may be variously assessed,
and are not likely to be understated, the evidence of the Beecher
Report showing that in the prevailing mood they may even be
pressed to the detriment of health or hygiene or other essential
public services.

Nor will a local education authority escape priority problems
as acute. Should backward schools be coaxed or axed? Should
quantity be cultivated, leaving quality to take care of itself?
Existing schools improved or new schools multiplied? "African
witnesses preferred not to discuss any priority other than the
immediate opening and aiding of more primary schools," but
the Beecher Report goes on to point out necessary preliminaries
to the fulfilment of these desires—improved and extended
teacher-training, which in turn involves extension of post-

primary education to at least the school-certificate level. How adjust priorities to redress the balance between the claims of girls and boys? How settle priorities between literary and "practical" subjects? Between ancient and modern methods of teaching?

These and many other brain-twisting problems await the Local Education Authorities and the Boards of Managers, and it is after taking them into account that the Conference registered its faith in these bodies, only stipulating that there shall be formal association of religious bodies with the established forms of administration as a guarantee of the type of education pre-supposed. One other plea is advanced elsewhere in the volume —"that the young educated men and women be given a fair share of authority, if necessary by nomination, for otherwise the older men will monopolise government and the young will become disaffected and discouraged." The warning is no doubt derived from and might well be taken to heart in non-African circles.

2. *The Unofficial Local Partner*

It will not be necessary to repeat, though it might be worth while to re-read at this point, what has been said in Chapter IV of the fourth educational axiom under the heading "Spiritual Roots", as also the section of Chapter VI dealing with the "Unofficial Partner". The latter's last quotation (from the Western Group's Report) lays down as a *sine qua non* the acceptance of partnership between unofficial and official "with open-heartedness, without reservation, reluctance or restrictions." If such acceptance is indispensable between central and local, it is even more so between local and local where occasions of stumbling are legion.

For voluntary agencies to adapt themselves to the local government set-up as described above involves some degree of abdication and abegnation. For local education authorities to reconcile themselves unreservedly to the partnership of voluntary agencies thrust upon them by statute may also involve some degree of discipline and effort to eradicate deep-rooted prejudice. To neither will it be just to impute ill-will, nor need the difficulties be exaggerated. It was the magnitude of the educational enterprise in all its breadth and depth which inspired the new perspective of the Cambridge Conference, and its discovery of so large an area of agreement; the same motives may be relied upon to inspire and maintain the spirit of local partership, even when subjected to severe testing.

Voluntary agencies it may be recalled are not a homogenous unit, and partnership within their own ranks presents its own problems. They include for example Muslims. With them there is no difference of opinion on the inseparability of religion and education. To quote the Muslim members of the Conference: "There are in British Tropical Africa many millions of Muslims who would be prejudiced against education if no adequate provision was made in the educational system for religious instruction. They look to the Koran for their spiritual uplift and moral guidance. Arabic is the medium through which they learn their religion. But it also opens to them a vast field of culture. . . . Wherever possible the existing Koran schools, provided that they teach secular subjects as prescribed by the education department, should be linked up with the normal educational system and receive financial assistance."

There is here an area of agreement, but it may be found difficult to live up to the ideal where Muslims find themselves under a predominantly Christian local authority, and vice versa. "In some areas there are competing claims between Muslim and Christian communities for the establishment of schools. This may become a political issue as for example in the Gambia and parts of Northern Nigeria, where Muslim opinion will be increasingly reflected in local elections." "In certain areas where there is a predominance of a particular religion or denomination, as for instance in the Muslim belt of Northern Nigeria, there may be need for special discretionary powers in relation to voluntary agencies to be accorded to local education authorities. If however this were to happen generally care would be needed, especially in predominantly Muslim areas, not to apply the principle *Cujus Regio Ejus Religio*." "There is certainly a feeling in Northern Nigeria that there should be less restriction of voluntary agency schools where there continues to be an unsatisfied demand for educational facilities."

There are other elements not altogether easy to assimilate

F

within the unofficial local partnership. "Many missionaries who come to work in British colonies are of alien birth, speech and upbringing, who have not grown up in the tradition of British institutions. They sometimes speak English very badly." There is more than one reference in the Reports to competition between Christian denominations. "An effort must be made to resolve the conflict between denominational teaching and good and economic planning." "Interdenominational rivalries are preventing essential reorganization." Difficulties have also arisen over "private" schools, provided neither by Government, local authorities or religious bodies—some conducted for private profit, some by non-profit-making associations, some tolerably good, some intolerably bad. Again, the conscientious convictions of the Roman Church as expounded in the Encyclical of Pope Pius XI in the Christian education of youth, are not easy to fit into a system of Government and local education authority schools which are not regarded as suitable for a Roman Catholic child to attend.

These references serve to acquit the Cambridge Conference of unrealistic optimism; their confidence in the future is not based on Utopian thinking. They also serve to explain some of the misgivings with which both official and unofficial partners may face each other. The former may be tempted to wish to eradicate intransigent elements in the interests of a neat and tidy uniformity : they may be inclined to react strongly against the former missionary monopoly and to under-rate the extent to which Christian voluntary agencies have outgrown their dependence on European Missions and assumed the character of African Churches. Christian voluntary agencies on the other hand may be inspired by no less understandable hesitations. In so far as they appear to be on the defensive it is certainly not because they want to perpetuate European control. "They have set up compact bodies of control, many of which are almost wholly composed of Africans. There is a great deal of excellent African leadership available in these bodies." It is rather that they are conscious of a trust. Theirs it is to secure that African children shall enjoy that "good growing weather" (as the gardeners say) which the glories of the Gospel and fellowship in a worshipping community afford. They are nervous because local education authorities may be predominantly manned by those who if not themselves biassed against Christianity may be swayed by those who are, or may acquiesce in diluted Christian teaching.

It was at first sight surprising that Christian voices were heard at Cambridge resisting the proposal that a Church school should receive 100% of both capital and maintenance costs from public funds. The Conference Group on Responsibility and Control rejected a proposal that "Churches should continue to pay part of the cost of their schools; but their reasons for rejecting it did not convince all members of the Conference: no general agreement was reached on this point." There was a genuine fear that Christians might find themselves no longer free to provide parents with the type of school they wished to have. Total dependence on what might become a totalitarian state would be dearly bought: indeed the delegates had not far to look for what happens when a Government decrees that nothing may be taught in a school that it does not like. Identification with Government might expose the Christian Church, if public opinion took a violent turn, to the kind of execrations hurled at Christians in China.

What reassurances had the Conference to offer to the unofficial partner? It must be remembered that it met before the African atmosphere had been embittered by more recent happenings in South Africa, Kenya and Uganda. If it had been aware of these events it might have conceded that the anxiety of those who were haunted by dread of totalitarianism was not wholly unreasonable, and even that the Chinese analogy was not so irrelevant to Africa as it seemed. But the policy of the Conference was adopted in the light of what all recognised as a revolutionary age; the totalitarian danger was not unfamiliar; racial tensions were the order of the day; everybody knew what had happened in China. An educational system must be developed that would stand the strain of any emergency; there must be nothing shoddy in its foundations. It must be rooted and grounded in religion. If that was to be achieved the entanglement of the Churches with the Government and the Government with the Churches, to which both were deeply committed without compromise of the autonomy of either, must be continued with all the courage and confidence of conviction, fortified by fundamental and frank scrutiny of the overwhelming issues confronting African education.

That is the reassurance that the Conference has to offer. It cannot be repeated too often that all were agreed—and the "all" comprised so many elements that unanimity was something of a miracle—that the religious character of the education given in Church schools must be preserved, but further that all education in schools must have a religious basis, which could only be assured if religious bodies were formally associated with government bodies in the control of education. "There must be full and ungrudging partnership between the voluntary agencies and the central and local government bodies, each partner recognizing the value of the other's contribution." No fewer than 25 out of 39 speakers in the final debate spent most of their time in stressing this.

"Dichotomy must be avoided at all costs" (the sharp division between State and Church schools familiar in the educational history of Britain). "There are two ways of avoiding a dichotomy: either one half can be cut out entirely, or the two can be fused. We strongly urge that the latter method should be adopted. This does not imply uniformity of management . . . but it does imply uniformity of treatment. The community should be able to take a pride in all schools as its own; it is all-important that this attitude should be established as soon and as firmly as possible."

If African Christians (and it is for them to decide) can respond to these reassurances "with open-heartedness, without reluctance, reservations or restrictions" it may open a history of Church-and-State, Official-and-Unofficial relations unparalleled anywhere in the world.

Chapter Eight

"EXPATRIATE" REINFORCEMENTS

THE future historian may well wonder whether in 1952 anybody liked being called an "expatriate." He will search in vain for its use anywhere outside Africa. Consulting his dictionary he will find that the word had associations with banishment, and banishment not always creditable to the banished; the renunciation of citizenship implied was often involuntary. The word as used at the Cambridge Conference had no such sinister meaning; it cast no slur on the European Government Officer, or on the missionary or the settler. It appears to have crept into use as being a less offensive term than "foreigner" and more inclusive than "European," to distinguish non-African from African. Politeness can be carried to absurd lengths, as when (not in the Cambridge Report) to spare susceptibilities wounded by such respectable words as "native" or "national" the African is dubbed "non-expatriate". Perhaps it will save our future historian perplexity if we ask him to forget the first word in the title of this chapter, and concentrate on the second. We will call Africans Africans, and all non-Africans co-operating in African education *Reinforcements*, whether serving in Government departments, or in Missions or in other capacities.

Apart from the negative merit of expatriating "expatriate," "reinforcement" has positive advantages. It implies the recognition that whatever strengthening from outside African education may need in a time of transition or emergency, its permanent stability and development must depend on its own African resources. The value of reinforcements will be conditional upon that recognition, both by the reinforced and by those who do the reinforcing. The latter will do harm if they come to regard themselves as indispensable and so stunt the growth of responsibility and self-reliance. The reinforced will suffer harm if they lean too long on others who make decisions for them—if they do not harness their nationalism to the gigantic task of rearing the citizenship of the new Africa.

Posterity is likely to ask two questions, one about attitudes, the other about functions. Were the dominant attitudes of all concerned with African education attuned to the note of reinforcement? Were the functions assigned to reinforcements within or beyond legitimate limits?

1. *"Priming the Pump"*

Reinforcements according to the Western Report are needed to "prime the pump." "You cannot have good teachers until you have good schools, or good schools until you have good teachers. In one way or another the pump must be primed. As a matter of history this has been done by missionaries and expatriate teachers, and they have made the progress of education, slow as it must often seem, far more rapid than it would otherwise have been. A country which has not the opportunity or the will to accept external assistance of this sort while facing the problem of building up an educational system from the beginning is condemned to a rate of progress which will be measured in centuries rather than in decades. The pumps at some levels will continue to need priming for many years to come if they are to get into full working order at a rate consistent with the urgent needs of the time."

This is unpalatable doctrine for those who, just because they are sensitive to the wider implications of education, are reluctant to accept help from outside. The Cambridge Groups on the expansion of education and on the teaching profession are prepared to incur whatever odium may attach to a policy of reinforcement. "Arrangements should be made to attract recruits from abroad by offering satisfactory terms of service, including a pension or superannuation scheme." "If expansion involves the necessity of recruiting more expatriate staff until sufficient trained Africans are available, they should be recruited." The word *until* should no doubt be graven on the heart of all reinforcements. It would save the recruit from the insidious habit of assuming his own indispensability, and would put him right and keep him right with his African friends.

2. Strategic Points for Reinforcement

i. Secondary Schools

What functions are recruits required to fulfil? The expansion which those quoted in the last paragraph had in mind related to "the provision of those stages of education from which entrants to the training colleges are drawn; and where existing training college facilities are inadequate, the expansion of those facilities should be the next priority." The Eastern Group is prepared to be dogmatic on the same point: "Expansion in secondary education must be based for the present principally upon an increase of the number of teachers coming to Africa from Europe. Such teachers are expensive, but in the early years of expansion essential, to the development of African education." (See p. 24 ff.)

An increase in the number of really good teachers should be the spear-head of educational progress, and there is no single aim on which effort could be concentrated to greater advantage. "The Secondary Grammar Schools must on the whole look to the universities for their teachers, and it is largely because the number of African graduates is so small, and only a minority of these take up teaching, that these schools are so dependent on expatriate staff."

ii. Training College Reinforcement

Teacher Training Colleges even if a second priority tread very closely on the heels of secondary education as claimants for reinforcement. The Conference "was depressed with the reports we heard of the difficulty of staffing teacher training colleges." In Chapter III, section iii. are quoted reiterated judgments to the effect that it is in the teacher training colleges that the ultimate remedy for all ills is to be found. Theirs is a major contribution. They are in a key position. Their plight, and the fact that so many are Church colleges enforce their appeal for recruits. But recruits must be picked men and women, experienced but skilful to apply that experience to new conditions.

"Grammar school experience in England is not necessarily help-
ful in training teachers for African primary schools." Their academic qualifications should be such as to command confidence,
but "need not necessarily include a University degree." Governments, we are told, are over-fastidious in insisting on graduates,
(half the teachers in British teacher training colleges are non-
graduates), and yet not fastidious enough in that "they are often
content with a graduate without enquiring if he is specially
suitable for teacher training college work." It is on sense of
vocation and high character that the Report lays its main
emphasis.

iii. Girls' Education

Not least in the Women's Teacher Training Colleges, and indeed in all branches of girls' education do pumps need priming.
"A great expansion of girls' education will be needed if territories
are to overtake arrears. We are aware of the urgent need to increase the number of women teachers." "For a long time to
come educational expansion among women and girls will depend upon the expatriate, whether she is employed by Government or Mission." Women now have to be recruited with an increasing variety of specialist qualifications, women abreast of
modern educational development, women skilled in home-
crafts, women with boarding-school experience, women with
some knowledge of those English Institutes of Education, which
the Conference is so anxious to introduce into Africa (not without modification) for the co-ordination of teacher-training.

3. The Supply Base

Recruits however are not the only means of reinforcement:
there is supply work to be done at the British end to reinforce
reinforcements. There is work to be shared out between the
Ministry of Education in Whitehall, educational experts, local
education authorities, school governing bodies and the teaching fraternity in Britain. Posterity is not likely to make allowances for the anxieties which haunted educational administrators in Britain in the 1950's—unwieldy classes, the need for
new schools and more teachers. But they will be extreme to
mark whether all was done that might have been done to meet

the claims of African partners by facilitating the release of teachers and by their re-absorption into the profession when their work in Africa was done. The Conference recommends a Standing Professional Committee of Educationalists in Great Britain to which colonial educationalists could turn for advice, with a bureau which would provide information and help about conferences on educational problems and refresher courses available for African teachers on leave. It is also suggested that interchange of teachers should be developed.

It was noted on page 30 that the Conference was impressed by the value of teachers' associations: it would like to see such African teacher associations (comprising all engaged in both the practice and administration of education), linked with the corresponding professional associations in Great Britain. The case in established for recognizing the solidarity of the teaching profession and making it a reality. Nothing would provide a more potent reinforcement of African education than the knowledge that its problems were known and shared by a teaching profession in Britain acutely alive to its needs, even to the extent of sparing an ample supply of volunteers for African service, cultivating the friendship of its products studying in England, and welcoming into its fellowship all members of the profession visiting England.

Lest it be inferred that nothing had been done along these two lines—the marshalling of experts and the consolidating of the ranks of teachers—until the Cambridge Conference, a word must be said first about the Advisory Committee on Education in the Colonies set up in 1923 "to advise the Secretary of State on any matters which he may from time to time refer to it, and to assist him in advancing the progress of education in the Colonies and Protectorates of Tropical Africa." The suggestion came from Dr. J. H. Oldham and the Conference of British Missionary Societies. The committee has brought to bear upon African education the corporate thinking of the best educational minds, and has exercised a decisive influence on policy. Over thirty years its sphere has extended beyond the African field, while it has been modified by the growth of self-government, and by the formation of two specialist bodies on higher education. The Inter-University for Higher Education Overseas, and the Advisory Committee on Colonial Colleges of Arts, Science and Technology. It has been responsible for producing many valuable reports, not least the Report on Mass Education. Without it the Cambridge Conference would not have come about, nor the deputations to West and East Africa whose reports provided its basis of discussion.

To the consolidation of the teaching profession successive annual conferences of the Overseas Council of the Church of England, and of the missionary societies have for ten years been making a contribution. They bring together those who are engaged in the practice and administration in England, Africa and beyond in a fellowship which realises in miniature what the Cambridge Conference hopes to see enlarged and universalised.

4. Reinforcement for Research

Research is a somewhat pompous word for the kind of investigations which the Conference wants to see undertaken. Seven topics are catalogued as worthy of attention:

   a. Problems of Girls' Education.
   b. Syllabus of Religious Teaching.
   c. Muslim Education.
   d. Selection for promotion; principles of assessment.
   e. The fresh approach to teaching methods.
   f. The contents of subjects in the curriculum.
   g. The teaching of English as a foreign language.

Recruits will have to live long in Africa before they can contribute much to this "research", but something distinctive they may have to give from their previous experience, and provided they do not forget until, their contribution is not likely to be unwelcome, and research may offer a rewarding field of partnership.

5. Literature Reinforcement

Literature does not keep pace with literacy. There is a famine in books. "Unless the range and amount of vernacular literature is vastly and rapidly increased it will be necessary to reconsider the whole policy of mass education." "The problem of the distribution of literature of all kinds is fundamental." "Literacy is only a tool, and mass education for literacy is wasted effort unless enough reading material can be provided as a follow-up."

It will be many a year before his or her knowledge of African languages or mentality qualifies the recruit for anything but a very junior partnership in any team of translators or editors; but junior partners have their uses and have even been found indispensable in this field, if only as stimulant and friendly critic. Such a partnership is in itself an enlightening education in all things African. There is no more exacting and exasperating work than translating ideas into new idioms, but there are no more enduring friendships than those which have originated in such collaboration.

6. Reinforcement and the Cambridge Axioms

Let us end this chapter by relating its subject to three of the four axioms expounded in Chapter IV.

i. Reinforcement for Adult Education

In the first paragraph of this chapter reinforcements are defined as including non-Africans co-operating in African education while serving "in other capacities" outside Government or Mission employ. We had particularly in mind a Conference reference to "most interesting and heartening developments among adult women. Increasingly European women are joining in voluntary efforts to improve standards of home-life for African women, and to bring them literacy, skill in crafts, and a training in how to run their own affairs. . . . It would be impossible to record either the extent or the variety of work done in all territories by individual women, wives of members of the Colonial Service, of planters, settlers, farmers, of men in banking, industry and commerce. They run clinics and infant welfare centres, play centres and crèches, schools and sewing classes, and in so doing build up the confidence of un-schooled African women in unfamiliar social services, and put future inter-racial co-operation on the sound basis of community of interest." Several speakers in the discussions recognised the importance of this voluntary help as a contribution to the building of the Africa-to-be. Social service on a voluntary basis is an English tradition which might well be injected into the tradition of secondary schools. "Where there is plenty of willingness to help among European women living in Africa, but some diffidence because they do not quite know how to set about it, efforts must be made to overcome this, and put those who are ready to engage in some special form of social work in touch with people of experience in that field." "European women have a great opportunity of doing effective work to help their African sisters."*

Reinforcements are also taken to include those in Government departments. This has a special relevance to the community-building work of adult or informal education. As was said in the course of discussion: "We must somehow get informal education carried on through the co-operation of technical people of different kinds. The days of the one-man team are over. We now have development teams, and the development school in which members of the teams who are already trained in their own technical lines come together to find out how they can most effectively co-operate. Community development can only be carried on through willing departmental co-operation." Training is essential. It in no way detracts from the voluntary and unofficial character, and informality of informal education, but rather enhances them when officers of government departments give "off-the-record" help in training these teams, bringing to bear their specialist knowledge of hygiene, housing, handicrafts or animal husbandry.

There is one subject that the Conference agreed could not be omitted from an educational system without failure to reach its objective, namely training in race-relations. "To produce a better understanding between men and women of different races is of particular urgency in plural communities." We do not think that reliance should be placed upon formal teaching about race-relations. Right attitudes are acquired almost unconsciously from association with teachers who themselves show in their lives goodwill to other people. They are learnt by pupils in the process of living, working and playing with pupils who belong to other communities."

---

* The Y.W.C.A. courses for those intending to live in the tropics are directed precisely to meeting this need, as are also the courses for laymen about to go abroad, organized by "Overseas Service" at Moorpark, Farnham.

Such an understanding will be a by-product of the co-operation of these volunteer reinforcements in the community-building work of adult education. Training in inter-racial relations is best acquired through the multiplication of inter-racial relations.

ii. Reinforcement of Agricultural Education

Inter-departmental co-operation is as much to be desired within the formal school system, as in informal education. But the Department of Agriculture has a special role. Is education rooted in the soil of Africa? was a question put in Chapter IV, and a fundamental axiom was formulated that rooted in the soil it must be, literally as well as metaphorically. There can be no more welcome reinforcement in the school than the agricultural officer who takes a personal interest in what farm and garden work is being undertaken, thereby encouraging individuals to realise the importance of such work to the country, and its fascination. Few Old Boys of Trinity College Kandy Farmers Club will forget Saturday mornings spent with the then Director of Agriculture in Ceylon, afterwards the renowned Sir Frank Stockdale, when he led the Club all over the College estate, discussing the pro's and con's of every plan and process, and playfully insisting on unattainable standards of accuracy in their answers to his questions.

iii. Religious Reinforcement

Finally we come to posterity's question about spiritual roots. Was education rooted in the soul of Africa? Here it is the missionary reinforcement that first springs to mind, and rightly so. But it would be betrayal of the main message of the Cambridge Conference if attention focussed exclusively on the padre or the Church college or school.

"Secular education is not enough. Our deliberations presuppose an education with a religious basis and a spiritual doctrine of human nature and destiny." That applies to all schools as is implied in other quotations in Chapter III. It is assumed that all reinforcements (due regard being paid to conscientious objectors) will associate themselves with this fundamental principle, whether administrators, executive officers of Government or teachers. Religious instruction is vitally important, but there is more to it than that. "To teach about religion is not enough. It must be lived out in the whole life of the school community." But the school community is not a thing apart; it is bound up with the whole community outside its walls to whose influence, for better or for worse, it is inevitably susceptible. Everyone therefore who in whatever capacity comes as a reinforcement of that wider community becomes a reinforcement or the reverse of Africa's religious education. Christian witness in the relationships of daily life, dedication to the service of the community, faithfulness in worship, these all consolidate, as their absence loosens, the spiritual foundations on which the new Africa is building. It is a solemn but inescapable responsibility.

How will missionary reinforcements fare in the judgment of 500 years hence? A span of time roughly corresponding to that which separated Augustine from Anselm—two great "expatriates"—and separates our own generation from William of Wykeham, Henry the Sixth and William Waynflete. Will the Cambridge Conference stand out as ushering in an age when African apostles of education forsaking all other occupations dedicated all their powers of mind and imagination to this one cause? When these African pioneers and leaders beckoned reinforcements from all quarters of the world to tide them over a great emergency? Will it be recorded that the Churches of Great Britain, the United States, Canada, Australia, New Zealand, India, rallied to the aid of the Church of Africa? That they picked out their least unworthy men and women to serve and love the youth of Africa, to help them to stand on their own spiritual feet against all odds, showing forth in their lives something of the splendour of the teacher's calling, of the calling of an ordained minister of the Gospel?

To different centuries are allotted different tasks, in architecture, art, literature, medicine, progress social or political: there is something of each in the task allotted to the twentieth century of rearing the fabric of the New Africa, upon educational foundations well and truly laid and storey by storey completed. It is a costly task demanding something of the austerity and discipline which in the Middle Ages moved multitudes to unite in building majestically to the glory of God.

Who has ever seen or who heard in all the ages of the past that kings, princes and lords, mighty in their generation, bowed their haughty necks to the yoke, and harnessed themselves to carts like beasts of burden. . . . Although sometimes a thousand or more of men and women are attached to one cart, so vast is the mass, so heavy the load—yet so deep a silence reigns that not a voice, not a whisper even can be heard. . . . All hatred is lulled to sleep and quarrels are banished, debts forgiven and the union of hearts re-established. Forward they press, unchecked by rivers, unhindered by mountains.*

* Abbot Haimon, quoted in Cecil Headlam's *The Story of Chartres*.

Supplement A

A Survey of 50 years of African Education

THE DEVELOPMENT OF EDUCATIONAL ORGANIZATION

AS we have seen the first schools were planted in African Colonies by missionaries. It was a good deal later that Government Departments of Education were established: Gold Coast, 1890; Nigeria, 1903; Sierra Leone, 1909; Kenya, 1911; Uganda, 1925; Northern Rhodesia, 1925; Nyasaland, 1926. The main functions of these Departments have been, not so much the running of Government schools, though these made their appearance later, as the supervision, co-ordination and improvement of all schools, whether maintained by governments or by the missionary bodies, and the assistance of voluntary effort by grants from public funds.

In thus leaving voluntary agencies to lead the way, and following originally to supplement and later co-ordinate and supervise their efforts, Colonial Governments in Africa were acting just as the British Government had acted in England and Wales. Both in Britain and in Africa, the result was a dual system of education, Government and Church schools existing side by side, and gradually being brought together into one system.

But there was one great difference between Britain and Africa in the matter of school organisation. When the Government entered the field of education in England and Wales, it did so by establishing local School Boards; and in 1955 in spite of Treasury grants and Ministry circulars, the day-to-day administration of education is still in the hands of local education authorities. But when African governments entered the field of education, there was no modern system of local government

96

ready to their hand. Their indispensable agent was the versatile and over-worked British district officer. The traditional native authorities concentrated their power in the hands of the old men, and did not regard Western education as an adequate substitute for grey hairs. Under the theory of indirect rule, the Government was supposed to educate the native authorities to assume modern responsibilities; but that was a long and weary business. Only gradually were Governments able to increase their staff and give the district officer the assistance of technical colleagues. For many years he was accustomed to rule his district single-handed. In addition to his normal routine of court work and touring, he regularly surveyed roads, checked post-office accounts, demarcated boundaries, and inspected forestry nurseries, agricultural demonstration farms, prisons, hospitals and schools, as he would cheerfully say, "In his spare time." It was an age of paternal government. The time had not come for local education authorities, and African Governments administered education from their central headquarters. It was as if the Ministry of Education in London were responsible for repairing a school roof in Durham, issuing new chalk and exercise books to a school in Dover, and granting an application for compassionate leave to a teacher in Llangollen, as well as for inspecting all schools, paying building and capitation grants to voluntary agencies, and paying the salaries of all teachers from one end of the country to another.

This centralized system had obvious weaknesses, but it worked better than might be expected. The school system itself was small, and Government provided only a small minority of the total number of schools. Every assisted school had somebody—it might be an African catechist or parson, it might be a European missionary—to whom the head teacher could go for help and advice, and above this authority there was the Church Synod or Mission Committee. Though the Government's director of education was directly responsible for inspecting the schools, his administrative responsibility for most of the schools was only indirect. For many years the voluntary agencies were busy in the laborious task of establishing new schools in areas where there was no great enthusiasm for education. It was not until the nineteen thirties, when there at last arose a clamant

African demand for education which the resources of the voluntary agencies could no longer meet, that the strain on the centralized educational administration became intolerable, and the establishment of local education authorities became not merely a matter of educational desirability, but a matter of urgent administrative necessity. All African territories are now working towards a system in which the local education authority will be the normal administrative body. As we have seen in Chapter VII the Cambridge Conference spent much time in discussing the relationships between the central Government and the Local Education Authority and the central Government of the territory.

Development of Primary Education

The spread of primary education in Africa has everywhere been hindered by the same difficulties, and in every territory the graph has much the same pattern: a long period of very slow climb, followed by a sudden rocketing. Distances were large, communications poor or non-existent. Funds were limited, teachers—especially trained teachers—were scarce, and over large parts of the continent, people on the whole did not want education. Many can remember the days (even in countries which are now vehemently demanding more education) when the district officer went from village to village instructing reluctant chiefs and elders that they were to produce a quota of children for the new school: "From you I want six, from you ten, from you twelve." By one such district officer it is related that he went to see the new school opened, and found that the villagers, being ordered to produce their quota of children "to be given to the Government for its school," as they themselves put it, had detailed the blind, the lame, the diseased, the dim-witted. He called the elders togther, and asked them, "Is it true that these are the children whom you wish the Government to educate?" They replied, "It is true." He rejoined, "Then these are the people whom you wish to be rulers and judges over your children; for the Government seeks to educate children in order that in the next generation it may have men from whom to appoint rulers and judges over their brethren."

A few days later he returned to the school, and found the cripples gone and the school filled with bright healthy youngsters.

The beginnings are bound to be slow. As the railway train and the lorry penetrate the bush, as trade increases, as people begin to move away from home, as mining and commerce increase and towns develop, as money begins to circulate and opportunities of paid employment increase, education begins to spread, at first slowly and then faster, until there comes a day when the people awaken to the advantages of education, and begin to demand more schools than the authorities can provide.

The following figures illustrate the remarkable changes that took place in the first half of the 20th century. Precise statistics for the earlier years are not available, but the general picture provided by those approximate figures is unmistakeable. In the Gold Coast, some twenty-five thousand children were enrolled in 1910; in 1930 there were some sixty thousand; in 1950 there were nearly three hundred thousand.

There are few territories in which we have figures as early as 1910 that can be safely used in comparisons. But for the period from 1930 to 1950 we can observe the changes, and in most territories that period saw considerable expansion. The enrolment during that period doubled in Northern Rhodesia, trebled in Nigeria, and quadrupled in Kenya. To put this into perspective however, we must remember that 1950 itself was an early year in a further period of expansion which is still in full swing. Already by 1953 the Gold Coast enrolment had increased almost by a further 50 per cent, so that in 1953 about eight children were in Gold Coast schools for every one in 1930, and about sixteen for every one in 1910.

Expenditure on education gives another measure of the changes that have taken place, but here again, we cannot make precise comparisons because of changes in the value of money, differences in methods of accounting, and difficulties in defining our terms. Some of these limitations are removed if we express public expenditure on education as a percentage of total public expenditure. This percentage gives some idea of what the territory is prepared to afford for education. About 1930, this percentage for most territories was about five to six per cent; in 1953 it was about ten to twelve per cent.

The Development of Secondary Education

Facilities for Africans to obtain secondary education are of course everywhere inadequate; at a period when no major African territory had yet achieved universal primary education, there could be no talk of universal secondary education. Secondary schools are still highly selective, and because of inequalities in the pupils' social background and foundation of primary education, the age range in the secondary schools is still too wide.

But the problem of improving the quality of the secondary schools is as urgent as the problem of expansion. There are two main problems here: one is to provide secondary education of more varied types, the other is to improve the efficiency of the schools within a given type. The first problem is simply that almost all African secondary schools are grammar schools; there are no secondary modern schools,* and African public opinion has hitherto declined to regard secondary technical education as genuine secondary education at all. The question of parity of esteem is even more acute in Africa than in Britain, and there can be no question yet of giving pupils of secondary school age an education suited to their differing abilities and aptitudes. Whatever the reasons for this limitation in the scope of secondary schools, it is certain that there has been no policy, either by Voluntary Agencies or by Governments, of restricting secondary to that of the grammar school. There have been many attempts to provide post-primary training of one kind or another with workshops and farms, but they have not gained popular support. No doubt one main reason for this climate of opinion is that especially in West Africa, where there is no settled European population, Africans observe that the European manager or administrator, with his grammar school and university background, has a higher salary and social standing than the European foreman platelayer or workshop superintendent. Another reason is that until the last few years, there has been but little industry in Africa, and therefore but little demand for African technicians. This is one of the respects in which Africa is now

---

* Though secondary modern schools, under that name, are now being planned by the Ministry of Education of the Western Region of Nigeria.

changing fast. Just as the demand of European firms for African clerks was a powerful stimulus to African primary education a century ago, so the demand for African technicians is now proving a powerful stimulus to African secondary technical education.

The second main problem is to improve the standard of the many African grammar schools which leave a great deal to be desired. There are some excellent secondary schools: some provided by governments, some by voluntary agencies, an increasing number constituted self-governing on the lines of the English public schools. But there are others which are ill-housed, ill-staffed, and . . . and ill-equipped, in which private proprietors, with resources quite inadequate for their task, are striving to cater for the public demand, if not for sound education, at least for an examination certificate. Since science laboratories and workshops are expensive, and qualified teachers of science and technical subjects are hard to come by, these schools are commonly the most narrowly bookish of all.

Since the end of the war, secondary technical education in Africa has been going forward with new hopes and new energy. The principal type of establishment is the trade training centre, the function of which is to lay the foundations of the training which is needed to produce a fully skilled craftsman. Pupils are recruited to the trade training centres after six to eight years of primary schooling, and they are required on entry to be literate in English. The trade training centre inevitably has its limitations. Even though many of them undertake ambitious projects, such as the erection of their own buildings and sometimes buildings for other uses, the servicing of motor vehicles, and the manufacture of furniture or light metal goods, they cannot give their pupils the experience necessary to make them into craftsmen capable of using their skill to the best effect in industrial conditions. The work of the trade training centres needs to be supplemented by a properly organized scheme of further training within industry. The usual system is to give pupils a three years course in the centre, followed by two years training within industry; the whole five years period is regarded as a continuous course, and a certificate is awarded at the end of it.

The trade training centres are the more important since there are few schemes of apprenticeship in Africa like those which are common practice in Britain. Only a few industrial establishments, such as the railway workshops, are big enough to be able to run large-scale apprenticeship schemes. But a more important difficulty is that the demand for skilled labour of any kind, and of any standard, is so great that learners in any trade leave their training long before they are properly qualified, and turn their small skill into cash. The trade training centres have to teach their carefully selected pupils not only technical skill, but a proper appreciation of standards of craftsmanship and a sense of responsibility towards industry. Many of their pupils will expect to pass the appropriate examinations of the City and Guilds' Institute of London.

In addition to the skilled craftsman, industry needs the semi-skilled worker, and in rural areas especially there is a great need for the general handy-man. The training of the semi-skilled worker is left to industry itself. The general handy-man is trained in establishments which perhaps may be called secondary in the sense that their pupils come to them from the primary school—though not necessarily after satisfactorily completing the primary school course—but can be called secondary only in this narrowly literal sense. Their course provides for instruction in such crafts as carpentry and house-building, elementary metal work and forging, and the making of tools and furniture, as well as traditional rural crafts such as thatching and basketry.

All this vocational training, whether of rural handy-men or of skilled craftsmen, is distinguished from the workshop and other practical work which is given to pupils in secondary grammar schools as part of their general education. Such work is at present given only here and there; it is to be hoped that in future it will be given more widely.

The Development of University Education

We have mentioned that as an educational system grows, its different parts must remain in balance with each other, and that secondary schools must lead to polytechnic and university if Africa is to produce administrators and professional men to guide its development. We have seen that in 1952 the African territories were making efforts to expand, then improve their secondary education. Were similar efforts being made to provide higher education in polytechnic and university?

There is effort and achievement to be recorded. Since secondary education in Africa was so largely literary, it was natural that university education should develop somewhat ahead of polytechnic education, for which so much less foundation existed.

In the British tradition, the Government's share in the establishment of a university is limited. We look to the Government for the legislation and formal charter necessary to establish the university as a body corporate, and for a generous measure of financial help. For the appointment of staff, the devising of schemes of study, the admission of students, the fixing of academic standards, we look not to the Government but to the university itself.

During the war of 1939-45, the British Government, realising that the development of higher education in the colonies was already becoming urgent, appointed a Royal Commission, the Asquith Commission, to review the whole question, while a subsidiary body, the Elliott Commission, made specific proposals for university development in West Africa. On the advice of the Asquith Commission, the Government invited the British universities to establish an advisory body, called the Inter-University Council for Higher Education in the Colonies (changed in 1955 to the Inter-University Council for Higher Education Overseas). All the universities in the United Kingdom nominated representatives, the only ex-officio member being the Secretary of State's educational adviser. The function of the Inter-University Council is to help the university institutions in every way: in practice it advises them on their building plans and on their plans for academic development, acts as their agent in advertising staff vacancies and making appointments, and nominates representatives to serve on their councils. A parallel body, the Colonial Universities Grants Advisory Committee, considers the financial implications. Grants under the Development and Welfare Acts are made direct by the United Kingdom Government, not indirectly through the African

Governments. Like universities in Britain, they receive block grants on a quinquennial basis. Their staff have security of tenure, their academic standards are under their own control and are checked by independent external examiners, they decide for themselves whom they will appoint to their staff, and whom they will admit as their students. And this autonomy, it should be repeated, is fully accepted by the Governments; the colleges have no need to crouch on the defensive.

In the conditions of Africa in the nineteen-fifties, the maintenance of high academic standards can only be achieved at an inevitable price; and it involves a danger which has to be guarded against. The price is that the student numbers will at first be small; the danger is that the African university institutions will become mere copies of English universities, and will be African in little but name.

The enrolment of students in 1954-55 was as follows:

University College of the Gold Coast - - 349
University College, Ibadan, Nigeria - - 527
University College of East Africa - - 448

These numbers were disappointingly small. There were several causes. Buildings were not complete, and there has been on occasion a shortage of residential accommodation for students. Some students who would have been very welcome have preferred to go to England for their university studies, even for their first degrees; it is understandable that parents who can afford to send their sons (less frequently their daughters) to a university should prefer London or Cambridge to Ibadan or Makerere, but less understandable that African Governments who have spent large sums on helping to establish and maintain their own university college should grant undergraduate scholarships from public funds tenable in England rather than at their own college.

But the main cause of the smallness in the student body is the shortage of suitable undergraduates. The University College of the Gold Coast had in 1955 more than a hundred empty student places which it could not fill. Secondary education in Africa is making rapid progress up to the level of the external School Certificate examination, but the development of the sixth form

level of work has been slower than was hoped. Here, as elsewhere in education, a vicious circle prevails. Qualified sixth
form teachers (especially in science subjects) are difficult to
obtain from Britain, and the schools naturally look to the African university colleges to supply them. But the graduates of the
African university colleges are in great demand, and only a
small proportion of them enter the teaching profession. As long
as this is so, Africa must resign itself to the fact that there can
be no spectacular rise in university enrolment. It is to some
extent a matter of priorities. If we assume, as we unfortunately
must, that there are limits to the numbers of teachers and other
educationists that can be recruited from Britain, and that sixth
form teachers are particularly scarce, it becomes a question of
how to use the limited numbers available. In the Gold Coast and
the Western Region of Nigeria, at any rate, it would seem that
the African Ministers of Education are giving most of their attention to the achievement of universal primary education,
with all that that involves in providing teacher training facilities and expanding the staff of inspectors. Important as the
development of the university colleges is, it is not felt to have
the urgency of the expansion of primary education.

It might perhaps be suggested that for a few years at any rate
the university colleges themselves might recognize this emergency by admitting students who had obtained a Cambridge
School Certificate. The standard of a university is determined
more by the standard of its graduates than by that of its entrants. But this would have its dangers. It was important that
from the very beginning the confidence of the British university
world should be won and held, and it was to be hoped that in
the very near future university teachers from Britain would
move with freedom and confidence backwards and forwards
between Britain and the young universities and university colleges in Africa and elsewhere. From this point of view it was
essential that the young colleges should be clearly defined from
the beginning as of University College status, and consequently
that they should take on no work that was not appropriate to
that status. And so for the time being the price has to be paid;
the university colleges in Africa are small.

The maintenance of high academic standards also involves

the danger that colleges in Africa, as the African university institutions, will merely be a copy of colleges in England. How is this danger to be avoided?

Here the University of London came to the rescue. Recognizing that the overseas colleges had two needs, first to maintain their standards, and second to devise schemes of study which were appropriate to local conditions, it established what it called a special relationship, into which it was prepared to admit overseas University Colleges upon conditions, the principal condition being that the overseas teachers should be approved by the University of London. The special relationship with London is a temporary arrangement, intended to safeguard the standards of the young colleges while they are establishing themselves. It is possible because the University of London, alone among British universities, has the power to award degrees to external students.

The special relationship is not a uniform scheme, but is arranged to suit the circumstances of each overseas college. The essence of the relationship is that the overseas staff and the London staff collaborate in modifying syllabuses to suit local conditions, and in setting and marking examination papers. Syllabuses may be modified slightly, as in replacing English earthworms by African earthworms for biology candidates; or they may be more radically modified, as in the history syllabuses for West African candidates, who should not be required to give quite the same attention to Thomas a'Becket as is required of English candidates. The collaboration between London and the African college in modifying syllabuses means that the University satisfies itself that the modification will not allow African students to slip through the examination more easily than their English colleagues. It means also that the staff of the African University College will be teaching a syllabus which they themselves have helped to devise and which they feel relevant to their pupils' needs. The examining will be directly linked to their teaching, and they will not suffer the frustrations of preparing students for an examination in the conduct of which they have no share. The staff collaboration is personal; staff from Africa take part in discussions with their London colleagues and staff from London visit Africa to help in the conduct of the examinations, particularly in subjects which involve a practical or an oral examination.

The African colleges were successful—more successful than some people in 1946 dared to hope—in attracting staff of the right quality in sufficient numbers. The Inter-University Council saw to it that nobody was appointed with inadequate qualifications, and had no hesitation in advising colleges to leave vacancies unfilled rather than make unsuitable appointments. The 1954-55 staff figures in the Gold Coast, Ibadan, and Makerere were 142, 126, and 100. A young college, whose students come from many different tribes and cultures and are all working in a foreign language, and whose staff are tackling new fields of study and research, needs a generous ratio of staff to students; but the academic staff of these three university colleges could cope with a larger student body than the colleges possessed, if only secondary schools developed to supply it. All three have faculties of arts and science and agriculture; and the three colleges have between them two institutes of education, institutes of social research, extra-mural departments, and faculties of medicine. Makerere has a faculty of veterinary science and a school of art. The University College of Rhodesia and Nyasaland proposes to open with faculties of arts, science, and agriculture.

We need not discuss the heavy financial cost, and the generosity with which African Governments have assumed the burden. As examples we may mention that the Gold Coast Government and the Gold Coast Cocoa Marketing Board gave over £5½ million towards the capital cost of the University College and £2 million towards its endowment fund; Nigeria's capital grants total over £4½ million and £2¼ million for the college endowment fund; the East African Governments have spent large sums in endowing chairs at Makerere. All the Governments make quinquennial grants for the colleges' recurrent expenses. It may be said that lack of means is no obstacle to any African's receiving a university education; there is a generous provision of scholarships.

It seems that if buildings and staff and money and the generous support of public opinion can make a university, the prospects of university education in Africa are bright. What is needed now is a freer flow of qualified students from the secondary schools into the university colleges that are waiting to receive them.

The Development of Higher Technical Education

The Elliot Commission on Higher Education in West Africa did not limit its attention to university development. It emphasized the need for higher education of a type that was not normally provided in universities; and it recommended the establishment of what it called territorial colleges for the provision of higher vocational training of many kinds. This idea has developed in later reports, notably those of an Inter-University Council delegation to West Africa led by Sir William Hamilton Fyfe, and separate reports on each of the three large West African territories.

The upshot of these reports is that a parallel body to the Inter-University Council has been established, called the Advisory Committee on Colonial Colleges of Arts, Science and Technology. The colleges with which it deals, like the university colleges, are not under the control of Colonial Governments but have a considerable measure of autonomy. They are conceived of as being comparable in status and complementary in function to the university colleges. They should provide all forms of higher technical and vocational training (including commercial and secretarial training) of a post-secondary but non-university character, and they should provide facilities for certain types of research.

In the technological field, the colleges of arts, science and technology should emphasise the practical approach and provide their students with the background of theoretical knowledge which will give them a greater understanding of the practical side of their work in commerce and industry. They should aim at providing skilled technicians capable of filling posts of responsibility on the production and maintenance side of industry. They should train non-graduate teachers for secondary schools and technical institutes, and workers in the the fields of adult education, social welfare and community development.

For some years to come the colleges will need to give not

merely technical education but general education in the arts and sciences to the level of Higher School Certificate. This is a temporary measure, necessitated by the slow development of sixth form work in the secondary schools. These colleges are facing the same problem which the university colleges are facing, namely the shortage of suitably qualified entrants. As we have already seen, the universities and university colleges have, generally speaking, tended to await sixth form development in the schools, conscious that their very existence was a powerful stimulus to this development. The colleges of arts, science and technology have less reason to wait. Although some of the courses they offer will be parallel to those of university colleges, not all will be. If for the time being they provide courses which in Britain are usually provided in schools, they need have no fear that they are prejudicing their academic standing. And the provision of such courses will greatly help the development of their higher training. Basic courses at Higher School Certificate level will be needed by students proceeding to non-graduate training as teachers for secondary schools, or to higher technological studies. As time goes on and more and more secondary schools develop adequate sixth form work for Higher Certificate, the colleges will be able to shed this branch of their activity.

The colleges will take women as well as men students and will provide where necessary special courses for women. They will be largely residential: partly to make possible the attendance of students drawn from an extensive region, partly to give their students the social and educational advantages of living in a residential college community. They will attach particular importance to the interweaving of technical education and practical training. This is effected in Britain by day release of employees to enable them to take part-time courses at a technical college, or by the "sandwich system" of alternating periods of several months of technical education in college with periods of employment in industry or commerce. With the great distances of Africa, the sandwich system will generally be much easier to operate than a system of day release. The colleges will take over some at least of the existing technical training courses provided by Government departments, such as the training of dispensers and sanitary inspectors, of agricultural and veterinary assistants, and technicians in mechanical transport for the railways. The close co-operation between college and employers under the sandwich system will make this transfer possible and fruitful.

The governing body of the college normally includes representatives of the various interests with whom the college is in close relationship. These interests clearly include the Colonial Government, especially the education department and—in view of the college's dependence on Government financial grants—the financial authorities: commerce and industry: and the university college. In addition, the Advisory Committee for Colonial Colleges of Arts, Science and Technology is represented on the governing body of the college, just as the Inter-University Council is represented on that of an African university college.

These are clearly delicate problems of relationships which have to be faced. There will be special difficulties in dividing responsibility between the College of Arts, Science and Technology and the University College, particularly in such subjects as engineering and education and extra-mural studies, where there is a danger of overlapping. There will be opportunities for close co-operation between the two types of institutions, not only by the provision of certain courses at one institution for those who have completed a course at the other, but also by the interchange of staff. Where both institutions carry on similar activities, they must agree to divide responsibility not in the light of United Kingdom practice but of the actual social and economic needs of the territory they both serve.

All this is a matter of policy: how much of it is accomplished fact? We have already said that the climate of African opinion has not been favourable in the past to technical education. The new policy for the development of higher technical education has been laid down since 1944. It results from the conviction of educationists in Britain that higher academic must be supplemented by higher technical education, from the widening of African experience during the war, and from the realization of Africa's industrial possibilities and her need for trained technicians.

Before the war, students of Achimota College, Gold Coast, entered for London university degrees in civil and mechanical engineering, but these university courses lapsed when Achimota was reorganized after the war, and have not yet been resumed by the new University College of the Gold Coast. Higher technical education in the Gold Coast is being given in the Kumasi College of Technology, which was established in 1951, and in 1955 had 660 students. In Nigeria, the Nigerian College of Arts, Science and Technology was established in 1953, and in 1955 had some 300 students. The Nigerian College is planned to carry on its work at three different centres: Zaria in the Northern, Ibadan in the Western, and Enugu in the Eastern Region. The Ibadan and Zaria centres were already at work in 1955. It will be some years before the buildings at Kumasi and at the three Nigerian centres are complete: but by 1955 the colleges were already giving courses of training in general arts and science subjects, engineering, building, commerce, agriculture, pharmacy, surveying, and teaching.

Sierra Leone possesses the oldest college in Africa, Fourah Bay College, established by the Church Missionary Society in 1827 and affiliated to the University of Durham in 1876. Fourah Bay was not taken up after the war and developed into a full-range university college. It retained its university classes, but was re-organized in 1950 into a college of Arts, Science and Technology. Technical and commercial courses were then added, and following the report of a fresh commission in 1954, the college will have its first professional course in engineering, existing buildings being adapted for the purpose. Fourah Bay had 350 students in 1955.

In Kenya, the Royal Technical College at Nairobi was established in 1954 by the East Africa High Commission. Like Makerere College, the University College of East Africa, it will serve all the British East African territories; and it is to be multi-racial. The buildings are to be completed in 1955 and the college is to open in 1956. By the beginning of 1955 the principal and the heads of the engineering, commerce and architecture departments had taken up their appointments.

These developments in higher technical education in Africa and elsewhere are expensive, and although the greater part of the money was provided by the Colonial Governments concerned, the United Kingdom Government provided assistance under the Colonial Development and Welfare Acts to the value of £1½ million between 1950 and 1955.

This section devoted to higher technical education is only half the length of the section devoted to university education, and the assistance given—so far—for higher technical education from heads voted under the Colonial Development and Welfare Acts has been only one-fifth of that given for university education. But these facts do not imply any measure of the relative importance attached to the two branches. They are so merely because technical education in the past has been less popular in Africa than academic education, so that after the war it was easier and more immediately popular to develop university colleges than higher technical colleges. But this will quickly change under the stimulus of the unprecedented economic developments which have begun in Africa since the war. It is significant that the Kumasi College of Technology, founded in 1951, had 660 students in 1955, while its colleague the University College of the Gold Coast founded in 1948, had 348. Africa needs both types of training, and they must work not as rivals but as colleagues.

Supplement B

DEVELOPMENTS IN EDUCATION IN THE
WESTERN REGION, NIGERIA, 1953-55

THE basis of all developments in education, which have taken place in the Western Region during the last three years, was the White Paper on Education prepared by the Minister of Education and approved by the Western House of Assembly in July, 1952. This proposed a big advance on all fronts of education but its main theme was the introduction of compulsory universal free primary education in January, 1955.

The year 1953 was spent in consolidation of existing programmes of primary, secondary and adult education and of teacher training. Much discussion of the new plan for 1955 took place at all levels—with local authorities, proprietors of schools, the Nigerian Union of Teachers, the Board of Education. Many details of the scheme for primary schools were worked out, including the control and management of schools, the provision and type of buildings, and the ratio of distribution of the new schools as between voluntary agencies and local authorities. This last was finally fixed at 60% for local authorities and 40% for voluntary agencies. A committee appointed to draw up a syllabus for the new six-year primary course worked throughout the year. A scheme for the gradual conversion of the existing eight-class school into one of six classes was also prepared. In January, 1953 Local Authority Teacher Training Colleges were set up for the first time in provinces and divisions. These provided a two-year course for the teachers who would staff the new schools in 1955. Voluntary Agency Teacher Training Colleges were also expanded at the same time.

Early in 1954 a scheme for the introduction in 1955 of Secondary Modern Schools was introduced and its details were worked out during the year. These schools were to provide a three-year post-primary course with a practical bias for such suitable boys and girls as did not gain admission to secondary schools. Fees were to be charged. The distribution of schools was to be the same as for primary schools—60% for local authorities, 40% for voluntary agencies. A team of educational experts from Hertfordshire County Council spent August in Ibadan in order to advise on modern schools and to hold a very successful re-orientation course for some 200 prospective modern school teachers. The Ministry held two further similar courses in 1955. Meanwhile much hard work was being put in on the primary school front. Early in the year, district planning committees, consisting of representatives of the local councils and Churches and others were set up to deal with the difficult problems of siting the schools and deciding their allocation, not only as between mission and local council but frequently between mission and mission. There were often bitter disputes and, where these could not be settled, the usual practice was to award the school to a local authority. Many areas had never had schools before and the objective was to ensure that no child had to walk more than three miles to school. These committees did magnificent work, especially those members who came from the Church agencies. There was much generosity on the part of the people in the giving of free sites, but in large towns such as Ibadan and Abeokuta suitable sites were difficult to obtain. After all this came the erection of the buildings which owing to the very large number of new schools required—some 3,000— had to be of economical type. The local authority schools were usually put up by local contractors with varying effect but many voluntary agencies supervised their own buildings with sound results. Never before had so many schools to be built in one year. Registration of children, for admission to Class I in 1955, took place in July, 1954: 400,000 children were registered. Of these approximately 385,000 were actually enrolled in 1955. The new primary school syllabus after thorough vetting by the National Union of Teachers and the Gold Coast Institute of Education was published in August, 1954. The first Regional Primary School Leaving Examination was held in October for some 50,000 children—a vast undertaking. A number of new secondary schools was opened during the year, most of them being community schools controlled by Board of Governors. Work in adult education (literacy classes in English and the vernacular) proceeded steadily. The Draft of the new Education Act, embodying the new provisions for primary, secondary, secondary modern and further education, and teacher training and dealing with the duties and powers of local authorities and many other matters was completed. At the end of 1954 the Government decided to drop compulsion from the primary school plan—educational facilities would still be provided free for every child but private fee-charging schools would be allowed to continue. The year closed in an atmosphere of expectancy on the part of those who had laboured so hard towards the goal of 1955. But elsewhere there were many Jonahs and many who derided the plan.

January 17th, 1955, was a red-letter day in the history of education in the Western Region. On this day universal free primary education began. The majority of the school buildings were ready, there was no lack of teachers, though many were untrained, and by the end of March 385,000 children had been enrolled. During the period May to August a survey of some 200 sample new primary schools throughout the Region was made. The Report of this survey considers that buildings are satisfactory in general, school equipment variable in quality and the supply of pupils' books adequate. Compounds are generally well kept and attractive but sanitary arrangements are more absent than present owing to no special grants having been made for this purpose. Trained teachers are doing well, especially some of the women, but there is a large number of untrained and inexperienced teachers: the living conditions of the teachers in waterside areas are poor. Group methods of teaching are in evidence but there is too much chorus work. Apparatus is satisfactory but the syllabus has not been covered in those schools which did not get under way until March. Children are clean, well-mannered and responsive and a healthy spirit exists in many schools. Attendance is quite satisfactory and the increased enrolment of girls is very encouraging. Most parents are keen and co-operative and local councils and Church congregations take an active interest in their schools—particularly the latter. This report concludes by claiming that the results of this survey of a cross-section of the region gives cause for reasonable satisfaction. About 250 secondary modern schools were opened in February and later. These did not prove very popular and attendance was very low in a number of schools. The rate of fee and lack of information about the aim of this type of school contributed to their unpopularity with parents. New secondary schools continued to be added to the list. On the technical side there was a large trade and occupational centre for men at Sapela in the Delta and two handicraft centres for schoolboys in Ibadan Town : others are to be built. A very important development during the year has been the preparation and training of the local authorities for the setting up of local education authorities. Many authorities now have their own education offices and in most provinces officers of the education department have been seconded to assist them. In October fifteen local authorities in Ibadan and Oyo Provinces simultaneously assumed the functions of local education authorities—a very important step forward. A large number of supervisors of schools have been appointed whose salaries are reimbursed to their employers by the Government. Broadly speaking there will be one supervisor in control of every forty schools. These supervisors of the various agencies work in co-operation with their own employers and the education department. A useful branch of the Ministry of Education is the Western Region Literature Committee which produces and publishes books and newspapers in the vernacular (one, a comic, is very popular) and also runs travelling bookshops for the distribution of books and school supplies. There is also the sound nucleus of a regional library which will develop into a full-scale library with its own buildings and trained staff. Children's libraries have been developed in some areas—notably Ibadan Province. The "Teachers' Monthly", produced by an editorial board of educating officers, has won popularity and enjoys a large circulation. Developments in the early future are a large emergency teacher training college at Ibadan, a women's occupational centre at Abeokuta, great expansion in adult education and a separate inspectorate (already being set up). Technical colleges are also envisaged.

During the three years 1953 to 1955 there has thus been a

wide expansion of the educational programme in the Western Region, particularly in primary education, where the number of primary schools has been doubled since 1954. There now exist approximately 10,000 primary schools. Secondary schools have also greatly increased in number. Teacher training colleges are now widespread, many of them belonging to the local authorities. Further education (adult) is to be largely expanded. Technical education is slowly developing. Local education authorities are being set up. The scene in January, 1956, is indeed very different from the picture of early 1953. Much has begun. More remains to be consolidated and improved.

Index